CW00509150

"James Hodson is one c
combines a passion for Go
skills. He has the heart of a ,
prophetic and evangelistic, combined with a fresh way c
bringing familiar stories to life.

There are many new testament commentaries, but STOP
AND LISTEN goes beyond the academic, and theological
approach to reading the gospels. Even though its
theology is sound, and James Hodson is at home in the
academic world, this is a refreshing, readable, and
challenging approach to familiar stories.

The keywords for this book are accessibility and
relevance. With a profound understanding of human
nature the writer Is able to place us in the context of
Jesus ministry on earth. The personal encounters
described draw the reader in, in such a way there is a
feeling of identification with each situation as it arises.
Richly illustrated from his own vibrant family background,
his professional career, academic training, and church
leadership experience, James Hodson has produced a
book that will be an enriching contribution in personal
devotions and as a group study guide for discussion. It
could also be used to give away to unbelievers. I
thoroughly recommend STOP AND LISTEN."
**Dave Fellingham, Church Leader, Author, Worship
Leader, Song Writer, Horsham, UK**

STOP & LISTEN

Learning to talk and walk with Jesus.

PublishU Ltd

www.PublishU.com

Acknowledgements

I want to thank my wife Julie, for her loving and consistent encouragement throughout this book. I couldn't have done it without you.

I want to thank Matt Bird and the other authors I worked alongside. Thanks guys, you pushed me when I needed it.

Contents

Foreword

I met James and his wife Julie at a church summer camp my wife and I were helping to run. At that time, they hardly spoke any French but you could tell they loved both the vision and the atmosphere of the camp. They were both very funny and brought a lot of good humour.

I found out later that one of the characteristics they liked most about our team was that we took time to listen to the Lord.

I'd learned to 'hear the voice of God' soon after my conversion. During a summer service training camp with Youth With A Mission, I discovered that these young people were 'receiving' revelations, words of encouragement or directions from the Lord. I was puzzled because I was not receiving anything. I almost went home frustrated. Then, little by little, I began to realise that God wanted to speak to me too, as in Jesus' words in John 10: 'My sheep hear my voice'. I understood that most of the biblical characters were people who were in direct relationship with the Lord: God spoke to them, they responded.

What could be more normal for a child to speak with his father and for the father to answer him. This practice of listening to God has become an essential factor in my walk with Him.

How God can and will speak to us is what you will discover in this book. If this is something new for you, it could transform your spiritual life and lead you to a new level of intimacy with the Creator of the universe.

A message to read, meditate on and put into practice!!!

Happy reading!

Daniel Schearer
Former Director of Youth with a Mission, France

Introduction

I have the privilege of working with a group of Jesus followers from across France. There's nothing special about us, nothing to make headline news. Yet we have three things I dearly love.

Firstly, everyone on the team wants to see the nation of France reached by the good news of Jesus. As one said: "If there are no French in heaven, who will open the champagne?" Secondly, there is an extraordinary amount of love, no sense of competition, just love. And thirdly, whenever we get stuck in a discussion we stop for a while just to listen. Silently listen. We're then invited to share what we've heard from the Holy Spirit. From there we try to find the path Jesus has set for us.

When you read this book, I'm assuming the first point for wherever you are. It is directed at people who want more for this world. This treasure we hold is far too good to be kept hidden. It was made for sharing. The last recorded command Jesus gave to his church whilst on earth, '... go and make disciples of all nations,' (Mt 28:19) lets you know how important that is. Swap the word 'nations' for the place God has put you into to help you get the full power of the statement.

The second point is essential but surprisingly rare. None of what we do is of any value if it is not based in love (1 Cor 13:1-3). It's patient, kind, keeps no record of wrongs, not easily angered and so on. Read on in 1 Cor 13 to remind yourself and bathe in its essential and life-giving beauty.

It's the third point that's the heart of this book. When Jesus says, 'and surely I am *with you* always, to the very end of the age,' (Mt 28:20) it was in the context of his project of an expanding Kingdom.

'The kingdom of the world has become the kingdom of our Lord and of his Messiah, and he will reign for ever and ever.' (Dan 7:27; Rev 11:15)

We were never meant to figure this life and mission out by ourselves. He would be with us, guiding, leading and talking. We need to stop and listen.

Shocked

I was deeply shocked some years ago when we were hosting a conference in Montgenèvre. We'd asked the question 'How many people hear the voice of God in their lives?' Less than 10% responded positively. 'How many of you have *ever* heard God speaking to them?' Still only a few of the room said they did. Most Christians there had never experienced a basic part of being a child of God.

Listening is an easily lost art. We hear words, but real listening is so much more. Living in France I'm often perplexed at how easy it is to misunderstand. In the days just after our arrival here, when we were doing any job to survive, I remember charging a lady 'dix euro' for a very quick repair job. She heard the word, 'zero', and pumped my hand vigorously, thanking me for my kindness. I didn't have the heart to correct her. She was so delighted I'd fixed her loo free of charge. She hadn't heard me.

The point

Hearing *his* voice well is an essential part of being *his* follower. This book is a short look at each chapter of the book of John in the Bible. It shows the place of listening and being connected with God as crucial to being the family he designed us to be. If there was a central verse, it would be Jn 10:27, 'my sheep hear my voice'. Although it's not attempting to be a full commentary, I do highlight this theme, using the text of the gospel. However, like trying to describe aerospace engineering to a six-year-old I'm fully aware that this book is in no way a full explanation of this amazing joy. As the writer amusingly said,

'Jesus did many other things as well. If every one of them were written down, I suppose that even the whole world would not have room for the books that would be written' (21:25).

I do pray that it will revolutionise your expectation of how you walk with Jesus, and how you hear his voice. How your '10 euros' doesn't become the accidental 'zero'.

How to get the most

I suggest that you start each chapter of the book by reading the corresponding chapter in the gospel of John. It will bring it to life, and hopefully make you fall in love again with the man at the centre, and above all, hear *his* voice.

The book will serve as a group study and chapters can be taken individually as well as a whole.

God always gets the final word.

John Chapter 1
I Found You!

Hide and seek is one of the best games ever. It has crossed generations, cultures and continents. I don't know what it is exactly, but it seems to delight young children. My own children and grandchildren have never asked me to stop playing the game, it's always me who says, 'OK last time!'. Even my four-year-old autistic grandson, who struggles with many verbal functions, has eyes that light up when the count 1, 2, 3 ... starts in that all too familiar hide and seek tone we adopt. He will frequently grab an adult to play the game by starting a count. Maybe it's because we like hiding! You know that short moment when you're all alone in some small cosy nook and no-one else can see you. Those few seconds before the cry goes out, 'I can see you!' can be quite precious and strangely delightful. Nathaniel was all alone under a tree. Was he playing hide and seek, probably not, but nonetheless Jesus said, 'I saw you'.

Like many stories the actual detail of what happened and why can get blurred. Why spoil a good story with the facts eh? However, in this first chapter of John it seems obvious that the writer is hitting some big arguments that are raging around the church family of his day. It is both heartening and discouraging to note that not a lot has changed. Our humanity never seems to fail in its ability to mess up, but then, and far more importantly, neither does God's ability to sort it out and to make things better than we could ever imagine.

God will always get the final say in this world.

The Word

With all guns blazing, John starts this first chapter by declaring that Jesus was everything. Many times, through the chapters he reiterates that he was not only the Son of God, but that he was fully God from the beginning (v1-3). Quite astonishing when you think about it, the creator of the universe living with us as a man.

Nothing has ever or will happen without him fully at the centre. However, the book does start with a slightly strange approach from our modern, western eyes, *the Word*. I wouldn't start a book to prove the divinity of Christ by talking about *the Word*. Thankfully my opinion was not required, and this turned out to be exactly what was needed then, and, importantly for us, today.

Before we embark on anything for God we need to understand in our heart of hearts, that *he* is the only real giver of life, and that this life which we enjoy comes about by him speaking. Simply put, he spoke, and it happened.

The story begins with him being the 'let there be …' and has continued through history and will do so through to the end. This includes all of creation and all he has planned to do. Even the death and resurrection of Jesus was told beforehand and was spoken and recorded down. Nothing is left to chance. As poor Job concluded after a torrid time, '… no purpose of yours can be thwarted' (Job 42:2). Our future and the end of this age has also been spoken and recorded. Though no-one may know when or even exactly how, the outcome is not up for grabs.

Daisy, our dog, sometimes sneaks into the car when we're about to go out. We may not even notice until we're pulling out and see her peering out from behind a seat hoping against hope she won't get thrown out. Isn't it great that God has not only called us into his home but has made a place for us?

None of the people who form part of his eternal family will ever say, 'Phew, I managed to sneak in here unnoticed'.

Hiding away under a tree

Having introduced the absolute all-encompassing might and magnificence of the Son of God we find that this power 'has become flesh and lived among us,' (v14). He needed to, as we'll see by the end of this book for some of the eternal purposes of God to be fulfilled. He also needed to for Nathaniel's moment of 'hide and seek'. I found you!

When Jesus meets him, he says, 'I saw you under the fig tree,' (v48). Fig trees have big leaves that are easy to hide behind. I know, we had one as I grew up, and it was very useful in my own hide and seek games as a child. We'll never know what he was thinking except Jesus did. To an amazed Nathaniel he says, 'you'll see greater things than this,' (v50-51). Whatever it meant to him, it was enough for him to get up, leave everything and follow Jesus as one of his disciples.

The word from heaven, Jesus the Son of God, knows where you are and what you're thinking. He wants to talk to you.

Your turn

Put your name or your group's name here............................

Repeat the following phrase, 'Jesus sees................................ when I think no-one can'.

Remember the context of the chapter. The one who sees you, not only knows you through and through but when he speaks, the words are more powerful and life giving than you can ever imagine. He made worlds by them.

This is why we need to listen.

In a later chapter, whilst Jesus was doing his best to get rid of freeloaders and experience junkies, he asks his disciples if they are going to leave him too. They reply, 'Where else shall we go, you *alone* have the words of *eternal life*' (Jn 6:68-69). They got it. He was the word and what he said turned on the lights (Jn 8:12).

Jesus' words to you and to your group have the authority and the power to turn your light on – to create, shape, change, breakthrough, anything and everything. In the list of priorities in our life (yes, we all have them) we must give space and time for *his* voice.

Nathaniel was never the same after Jesus spoke to him. Jesus' words to me have shaped, directed and led me to where I am and despite my ability to mess things up, they remain the central focus of my life. They have come to me personally, through others, in my group, in the Bible and in life. As the chapters unfold, we'll see many of the ways in which he speaks and the effect it has.

Our Response

Nathaniel's response to Jesus' words was to accept the call to follow him. Tradition holds that after Jesus left, he travelled to India and then Armenia telling people about his wonderful Lord and healing them, for which trouble he was flayed and beheaded. I don't suppose he's too bothered about that last bit now, apparently it doesn't compare with what's to come. (2 Co 4:17)

So, for you, the reader, be aware that the same Jesus who came from the Father and is himself, Almighty God (Is 9:6) is the same Jesus who sees you and, like Nathaniel, has the words that not only give life but are directed specifically for you.

Our character is shaped by the company we keep and though life's pressures often crowd us, wherever it is, find your place to be with him. For me it's my morning walk with Daisy, our dog. I guard it fiercely not because I'm very spiritual but because I know that without his word into my life, I quickly descend into messing things up again. With the telephone on silent, the majestic mountains in which I live and talking to Jesus, are part of my life blood now. Make his word, his voice, part of yours.

JAMES HODSON

Jodie had been listening attentively to the Alpha course she was part of. It was a course designed for those who wanted to know more about God. As someone searching, she was not yet sure that Jesus would speak to her. She was encouraged to try him out.

That Friday at work there was a competition to see who could grow a bean the fastest. She said to God, if you're there, let my bean grow the fastest. The staff all went home for the weekend.

On the following Monday, as the staff arrived at work, Jodie's bean had grown 3-4 inches. None of the others had even sprouted. She knew from that moment that God was real and would speak to someone like her. She gave her life to follow him.

God's joy is that we enjoy him and each other.

John Chapter 2
The Wine or the Whip?

Let's be honest, we rarely have any idea of what God is going to say or do. He seems to like it that way. He allows us to get into impossible situations, then, waiting until we're at our wits' end, the big reveal happens. Why couldn't he make it easier?

Here's why. God being all powerful, all knowing, all present — really means he's not in need of our help. No, in fact, he's never been looking for **our help**, he's always just been looking for **us**. This chapter finishes with the telling sentence 'He knew what was in the heart of each person' (v25). He knows you through and through and yet he's still looking for you. It's you he wants; the rest is just a way of getting you closer.

Cutting the grass

In our earlier years in France, we used to cut grass in the summer to help pay the bills. You could hardly call them lawns, more like patches of plants and grasses grabbed from the mountainside for a few years before nature reclaimed them again. One summer my daughter was out with her family for a stay. My grandson Boaz came out to help me cut a neighbour's lawn. I had my fully motorised powerful machine that sliced through any and every obstacle. Boaz, still under two, appeared alongside me with his fully automated, lightweight and completely useless plastic toy push-along that was now doubling up as a grass cutter. I showed him what to do and he copied me carefully, studying my movements with an attentive eye that surprised me for such a little chap. Up and down we went together and didn't finish until the lawn was cut. I don't know how he felt but judging by the grin on his face he enjoyed 'helping' me.

Me? I was nearly delirious with delight. Spending time with this bundle of joy was all I cared about. Had he actually cut any grass? No. What was important was that we'd done it **together**, and the fact he thought that he'd helped on a serious and difficult task, made me all the happier. Of course, in God's unlimited power, he makes our 'toys' into real machines, but that is for another book.

Do you have any idea how deep the Father's love for you is? How intensely he loves to be with you? His greatest joy is not that you've 'given your life to him' (it belonged to him anyway 'all souls are mine' Ez18:4) but that you're on the journey to be close to him. His joy is that we enjoy him and each other.

Maybe this is one of the reasons why he has programmed a life for us where we work together with him. Maybe all our prayer, our fasting, our great declarations, our evangelism, our giving etc are no more than a toy mower next to his real grass cutter. God never wants our effort; he wants our heart.

Let's look at two situations that come up in this chapter. The first player is a groom, and the second I'm going to call Rodney (not because it's his real name but he can represent all that's going on in the temple that day).

The Bride and Groom

I'm guessing that there were two options for this wedding Jesus was at, as to why it ran out of wine (v3). I'm mentioning the groom's family and not the bride's as it was their job to provide for the celebration, to make sure everyone had enough to eat and drink.

First idea: the groom's family didn't have much money and were hoping people wouldn't drink too much or just preferred the local water. Not sure that was realistic given the Jewish tradition for great wedding parties. Or secondly (my preferred option), was that the groom and his mum were carefree and happy and just invited too many people. I can hear the dad (who probably ordered the wine) saying, 'Now listen, we've only got enough money to pay for a hundred guests. Don't go inviting everybody.' I'm guessing they didn't listen. I get why Mary, Jesus' Mum, was there, and then, of course, Jesus, but why invite his twelve followers who you don't even know?

Maybe everyone they met got a 'Hey you've got to come to our wedding, it'll be great!'

'What? You've got visitors? Well bring them too!'

Maybe there was something about a spirit that wanted everyone to come that God liked.

Do *whatever* He tells you

So now, put yourself in their shoes when the wine runs out. What do you do? The old trick of taking off your uniform and mingling with the crowd won't work because your family are the hosts. You're the ones on show. Call the off licence? No, the money has run out and anyway, they're always shut when wedding feasts are on. Anyway, you'd probably invited the owner who was well into the party groove. So, next idea, ask the neighbours? – no, you've invited them all to the wedding.

There's no-one left to help.

Here's where Mary, Jesus' mother, has learnt a thing or two. Having been rebuffed by Jesus when she posed the problem to him ('woman, why do you involve me,' v4), she says the following words to the servants that should be engraved on the heart of every follower: **'Do whatever he tells you'.** How simple is that! She was not put off by his seeming disinterest, because she knew him.

The servants did exactly as he said (v7). The wine (around 800 bottles by most estimates) was tasted by the master of ceremonies who exclaimed (v10), why are you serving Chateauneuf de Pape now when we've only had Plonk de Plonk before? (I live in France, so it has to be French!) Now that's a party! Now that's life.

Did you really hear him and did you do it?

For the above method to have worked they *had* to hear what he said and then *do it*. You need to be *listening* and then be ready *to do*. Imagine the servants (alright now we know the family were not that poor!) saying, 'What a ridiculous idea! Why on earth would we do that? Those jars are for ceremonial washing, not drinking. No way!'.

Perhaps Jesus specifically chose the servants as they were used to doing what they were told. Others of us may well have kicked up and guess what? Yep, no miracle. You need to be ready to do what he says even when it makes no sense. Remember he's getting your attention as well as solving a problem.

He has tied his sovereign hand to working with us, even though we may only have the plastic mower. I would love to have seen the groom, the bride, the family, the servants.

What fun! What joy!

Rodney the money changer and Dove Seller Extraordinaire

The heart is all important if we're going to come close to Jesus.

A wedding celebration that would seem to offer no great 'spiritual' service got a party it would never forget, yet the guy trying to make an honest living selling animals to visitors so they could sacrifice to God and worship correctly, got a whip (v14-15). No miracles for Rodney and the other workers, just a scolding from Jesus, 'Stop turning my Father's house into a market' (v16).

Reading the other versions of this event and some of the history around it, it seems clear that to be a temple money changer, you were onto a good little earner. People had no choice but to use the money changers as there was no-where else you could get the temple coin. The animals? Well, who knows what margin they put on those but suffice to say it was a good living. The reality, which Jesus knew, was that it had nothing to do with worship or prayer.

The utter mess of overturned tables, his livelihood all over the ground, an angry man brandishing a whip; it must have been carnage.

Jesus knows what's in our hearts

Jesus knew that Rodney's heart was far away, more concerned about his life and his living than about God. The veneer of a spiritual job couldn't hide his real motives.

Jesus knows what's in our hearts. There's no hiding. You can't pretend to be anything you're not with him.

Sad Rodney. Somehow that mix is ugly and is the only recorded time that Jesus used violence to carry his message. There were no miracles for Rodney and the other sellers, only an angry Jesus, reclaiming his Father's house.

I wonder what he thought when he caught the gossip about the amazing eight hundred bottles of wine Jesus had miraculously drummed up at the wedding.

To finish

If we want to hear God, let's be like the little lad Boaz above. Just be happy to be with Jesus. Don't make great promises. Please, oh please, don't go all religious on God, He seems to hate it but do open up your heart. He knows it anyway and honesty is always the first step with God. It'll be your route to water turning into wine around you.

Listen carefully. And then, '***do whatever he tells you***'.

Josh was with a group in Mozambique as a young 17-year-old. He was being taken around the slum area of Pemba with a guide and they were brought into a home. Each person was introduced to the family who lived there. When it came to him, the guide said, '...and this is Josh the Prophet.'

All eyes turned to him. Me, a prophet? Help!

A panic prayer went up. The only thing Josh got from Jesus was a picture of a sparrow diving through power cables. Being a wise young Christian, he asked repeatedly for more information or an interpretation. Jesus simply said, 'just give the picture.'

He did. The whole family immediately erupted in tears. It was evidently something very important to them.

To this day Josh has no idea what it meant. He just listened and did as he was told.

Believing is learning to love.

John Chapter 3
I Just Don't Get It.

My wife is an artist. She has done a lot of figurative work, but her juices really flow when she goes into the abstract world. She'll often ask me what I think at the early stages of a painting. Being a husband, loving her to bits and not wanting to sleep on the sofa that night, I never say: "I haven't the foggiest idea what you're doing." However, despite the fact I might be enjoying the colour use and vague shapes, it's usually true. On top of the mystery is that our living area is often full of paint, canvasses, turps smells and brushes. Even making a cup of tea you're likely to come away covered in weird and wonderful oily colours. However, as all the shapes, textures and shades come together I'll go, 'Wow!'

My current favourite is a three-piece painting called a tryptic with blue and white hues that she gave me for Christmas. They are mounted side by side in pride of place in our living area. People still come by and decide that they must represent some Polynesian island, but I just love it for the life and joy it brings.

The night-time visitor

Jesus is so often like this. Poor Nicodemus came to him at night (v2), I guess he wasn't that keen on being seen. As a wise and respected 'teacher of Israel' he wasn't supposed to be the one asking questions he was meant to be giving the answers. I'm sure his secret will be safe.

It's not as though the conversation has been captured in one of the most famous, well-read chapters of the bible. Wait …

Despite Jesus giving full answers to Nicodemus about what was needed to see and enter the kingdom of God, he still couldn't get it. How can someone enter his mother's womb a second time? How can this be? (v4-10).

Have you ever felt that you just don't understand? With some great preaches and study we might start to get some of this chapter but imagine being in Nicodemus' shoes. Imagine being rated one of the cleverest people around, someone who had all the answers and yet you don't have the faintest idea what Jesus is talking about.

This can happen when we listen to Jesus. He doesn't always make things very clear. I've struggled with two verses in the same chapter we're reading, 'he didn't come to condemn the world but that the world might be saved through him' (v17), sitting next to 'whoever does not believe stands condemned already because he has not believed in the name of God's one and only son' (v18). One seems to talk about everybody, and one makes a division between those who believe and those who don't.

Listening is not always easy. Don't worry, it's not meant to be.

Why the difficulty?

Listening to Jesus isn't like a manual you have when you're building a flatpack from that furnishing company.

Rather it's like falling in love with someone. It's mysterious, it's wonderful, it's not easy but it's amazing.

I know that I should compliment my wife's hair when she comes out of the hairdresser and should notice the new clothes she's bought. We get to learn what's called the 'language of love'. I buy my wife flowers because she loves them; if my friend bought his wife flowers it would annoy her as a waste of money. I've learnt that her saying 'I'm fine' may not mean anything of the sort. I've learnt that her biggest language of love is us spending time together – but not being too intense. Shopping together is enough. She has learnt the things that fill me with joy, and she does them.

It is a journey that has enabled us to prize our marriage, not that we are perfect, but we are on the road. And it's the very journey that has made our life together so special. When Jesus is speaking to us, he's working this language of love between us and him.

Believing is learning to love

To say, 'I believe in Jesus' (v16), to get baptised and follow him (v22), to say 'he must become greater, and I must become less' (v30) etc can be meaningless if you're following some kind of flat pack instruction kit. For me believing the bus is coming in twenty minutes means I'm getting dressed, making sure I've got my wallet and walking off down to the bus stop. Sitting at home saying 'I believe the bus is coming' is meaningless if I need to get somewhere.

So, it is with believing in Jesus and listening for his voice. Verse 27 puts it so powerfully, 'a person can *ONLY* receive what is *GIVEN* them from heaven;' means that nothing I have outside of God has any value in his kingdom (now that's a brain twister). That means, I will make time to find out what his 'love language' is and do it. He already knows yours, which is another good reason to listen.

Given that Nicodemus openly came with Joseph of Arimathea to collect the body of Jesus after his crucifixion and take it through the Jewish burial process of spices and oils (using far more than was usual), shows that he was deeply moved by Jesus. Through all the puzzle, Jesus had become his Messiah.

The spillover effect

Whilst Nicodemus might have gone away still puzzled by the encounter, it laid the ground for a much-loved and well-known verse in the Bible – John 3:16. *'For God so loved the world that he gave his only begotten son that whosoever should believe in him should not perish but have eternal life.'* God's talking to us is rarely just for our benefit, it's for the world we're in.

Our misunderstanding, our getting it wrong, our total confusion cannot stop the will of God from achieving what it sets out to do. (Is 55:10-11) In fact, Nicodemus' confusion has led to the comfort and strengthening of millions of us over the centuries.

It's a doing thing ...

Does this mean we just don't bother trying? Not at all. Asking questions, finding out, pursuing answers even if we don't get it is SOOOO worthwhile. Not to do so would be like a homeless person throwing away the key to a new house they'd been given and going back to their cardboard box because they doesn't understand how to unlock the front door! Four times in this chapter the key in your hand has a name, 'believe' (v15, 16, 18 and 36).

Believe the key in your hand will open the door, not by putting it into your back pocket and doing nothing, but by putting it into the lock, turning it and walking into the house Jesus has made.

Belief here is the Greek word 'pisteuo' (closely related to the word used for faith). It is a verb and I still remember that means that it is a doing word. Believing means doing.

(Just to say my Greek classes at college were where I honed my skill of looking intelligent without having the faintest idea what the lecturer was talking about. My favourite comment of his was when he dropped in that most preachers who quoted Greek in sermons, in his experience, got it wrong. I felt let off the hook from my linguistic muddles. To this day, my favourite Greek remains the man who runs our local kebab shop.)

Get up and go

Pick up your key. Open the door. Like Nicodemus, make sure you come to Jesus even if it's at night, ask all the daft questions you want to, and wait around for the answers. Even if you don't understand them at first or seem to hear nothing, like Nicodemus he will change your life and bless the world around you in the process.

Lord, speak to me. Let me hear your voice. Show me where to look.

Bo was nine when God told him it was time to get baptised. He was on the Isle of Skye for a few days with his family.

He spoke to his parents and his uncle and aunt, whose home they were staying at. They agreed it could be done and as they lived by the sea, it would not be difficult to find where.

When news got out, four others came forward to be baptised as well as Bo. This included a sixty-year-old man who God had been talking to for some time about taking the plunge.

A nine-year-old boy's listening and his obedience opened the door for Harry to do the thing God had been nudging him on for years.

He goes out of his way to get into your way.

John Chapter 4

Keeping Jesus at a Distance

I remember being amazed at my children's hearing as they grew up. The natural filters that they had were quite extraordinary. I had no idea that humans had such abilities. You could call out loudly and clearly, 'Whose turn is it to clear the table?' and you'd get silence as the response. We lived in a fairly small house, so it wasn't a problem of distance. The words just did not penetrate their ears or, if they did, they were quickly smothered by the 'I don't want to do any work' brain brigade (like the white corpuscles designed to kill any unwanted intruders). However, quite remarkably, if you dropped your voice to a quiet hush and said, 'There's ice cream in the kitchen,' there would be a rapid thunder of feet and three eager faces would suddenly appear. The tiny receptor hairs in the ears had managed to lock on the words 'ice-cream' and 'kitchen'. They were ably helped by the inbuilt word amplifier lodged in each of their heads that was specifically programmed to activate at words like 'ice-cream', 'sweets', 'movie night' etc.

I never learnt this phenomenon at my human biology classes at school, but I can assure you it's true.

The woman from Samaria in this chapter also seemed to have a number of biological anomalies. However, these I recognise because I've used them frequently. I'll put them into four categories: debate, demand, deflect and, finally a fourth, declare (notice the clever preacher's use of 'Ds' there?).

Going out of your way to get into the way

Going through Samaria, whilst being the shortest route between Jerusalem and Galilee, was not the usual one used by Jews. If Galileans were despised in Israel, Samaritans were hated. You avoided them at all costs. Yet Jesus *had* to go this way, he got there at noon when no-one would be around, and he was tired (v6). We get that in France. The world in our area stops at midday and we're tired, hungry, and thirsty.

I'm guessing his disciples had gone off to a Samaritan town to buy food, because that's what you do at midday. All is quiet.

No! Wait, someone is coming. What, a woman? At midday?

Many say she probably came at this time of day as she was shunned by the other women because of her reputation. Normally you'd go at the beginning or the end of the day. Not for her, not today.

Everything was wrong. A Samaritan, a woman and a bad reputation. No way would she be of any interest to a Jewish messiah.

However, Jesus is in the right place, at the right time and with the right person. His Father wanted him there (v34).

Words of eternal life were about to come from his lips; life-changing and powerful for the millions of no-hopers in the centuries to come.

Did she receive the words Jesus said, welcome them and go for it? No, Jesus had to go through the three defences we so often put up when he speaks to us. They often flow together, like a whole body of armour we use to resist God.

The human armour: debate, demand, deflect

A simple request for a drink of water brings out the classic defences. Rather than answer the question she wants to know why Jesus is talking to a Samaritan (v9). Jews/Samaritans —today it might be Jews/Palestinians, French/English and so on.

We live on the border with Italy and for the last six years have had a steady stream of people coming looking for safety or simply a better way of life. When they ask for the proverbial 'cup of water' it is interesting how many locals respond with 'but why come to France?' Many thankfully do provide the glass of water and much more.

Jesus presses on with a powerful declaration of who he is and what he can do (v10). The woman is still locked in her own problems, drinking water and an easy way to get it. Rather than fall on her face and say 'Wow! You're the Messiah!' she wants to know how Jesus will meet her need for water (v11).

How often do we do this when Jesus is talking to us? Locked into our immediate needs we only think of life in those terms. We only want answers to our immediate problems. Like an infant at Christmas, we get obsessed with the wrapping rather than the present. I've often said that an empty wrapped box will provide more joy for an infant than any present you buy them. Save your money!

Jesus presses on. Verse 14 *'whoever drinks the water I give them will never thirst. Indeed, the water I give them will become in them a spring of water welling up into eternal life'*. Wow, oh wow of wow! This is the stuff that movies, books and crazy adventure stories have been written about. Here is someone offering it to *me*, a no-hope, lost woman from a despised community!

The shekel had dropped (or the penny for us). She gets that this is a little more than your average drink of water. Jesus' bulldozer has got through.

She can't quite separate her own personal needs of a daily trip for water from the magnificent promise Jesus has just made. How often do we do this? When we hear God, we so often relate it to an immediate need we have, the unpaid bill in the cupboard, the illness that's laid us low, our work. He's so often talking about something bigger and so much more important.

Isn't it sad in our prayer requests that we so often get stuck in our immediate needs; money, health, work problems. I call these level 1 requests. Do we often go to the next level? Help me be a better father/mother, help me bring Jesus to my neighbours. Even less frequently is level 3, 'give me a desire to follow you with all my heart,' or 'let us understand your will for our church', or ' let us make you look good. As Jesus said in verse 48 'you people will never believe unless you see a sign,' we're too often satisfied with a new bit of sticky tape on our cardboard box rather than going for the house.

The wrecking ball

Jesus brings out the wrecking ball for this woman.

The subtler approach has not got there. 'Go get your husband' Bang! Got her where she has been hiding – behind a broken and deeply shameful life. 'Sir I can see you're a prophet,' (v19) is one of the great understatements in the bible. In fairness, what do you say when Jesus exposes your life so completely. She deftly tries to step aside from the issue and move it back onto debate (v20) (here comes the deflect part).

At three, my son Joshua hated being stared at. Sometimes I did it just because I loved him to bits, other times it was to ask who'd fed toast into our VCR player. His now immortal line of 'wha dat?' whilst pointing anywhere but to himself was his vain attempt of moving the spotlight onto something else. Surely the lightbulb on the ceiling is of greater interest?

Well, why not? It's very uncomfortable when Jesus looks right into our souls! Why not try to get him onto a 'wha dat' moment and bring up some other debate?

It didn't work. Jesus was closing in, not just for her sake but his Father wanted the entire local city to know him; she was the key.

If you've had one of those moments where God is relentlessly breaking through your debates, your demands, your deflections, and you feel undressed and undone, cheer up, he has a much bigger plan than simply sorting you out. The woman goes onto the fourth D, 'declare'.

Is he the Messiah?

She doesn't go back and say, 'I've had a great revelation about the messiah, come and see him'. She is well known in the town and so says, 'come see a man who told me everything I ever did, could this be the Messiah,' (v29). It is so much better when we are honest when telling people about Jesus. We are never there because of our wisdom, we're there because he's revealed himself to us and what's more, he's spoken to the depths of our lives. All we really have to say is that 'Come and meet a man who knows me! Could this be our Saviour?'

There is nothing we have discovered by our own ability. We have what we call a 'revealed' faith. God came to us. We didn't go looking for him, we couldn't, we were dead. (Eph 2:5) Don't become a higher spiritual guru who expounds the great mysteries of the universe and looks down condescendingly at the mess around the world. It's a lie. I know it personally.

As the old tent maker said (1 Tm 1:15) 'Christ Jesus came into the world to save sinners, of whom I am the chief'. Like the doomed sand defences on the beach that our family loves to make, the tide of Jesus' words and love are unstoppable.

Finally

When the disciples returned clueless as to what had happened, little did they know that they were about to experience the only town-wide move of God recorded in Jesus' ministry.

Julie's business was in trouble. Through some government rules and an awkward local inspector, her company had been forced to join forces with another party she was uncomfortable working with. She wanted out from the business relationship which felt compromised but was unsure how to move forward.

God spoke to her husband and said that it was OK and it was in hand.

The next week the other partner said he wanted to move away and would she take on the company, which included the necessary certificates. It was not a difficult decision for her to make.

God spoke and it happened.

Do you want to get well?

John Chapter 5

House of Grace or House of Disgrace?

Chapter 5, despite including a profound healing that took place, is quite sad. It painfully contrasts the greatness of our Jesus to our human response. The word *believe* appears seven times in the verses yet six of them are in a negative context. The seventh was a life changer for my family, so I'll dip into that later.

The healing talked of doesn't end with a new disciple but rather Jesus defending himself and his mission. The context is also a little bizarre. The pool where the man was lying was called Bethesda. Looking into the Aramaic and Hebrew roots of this word it can either mean 'House of Grace' or 'House of Disgrace'. The legend went that an angel came down and dipped his wings causing the waters to stir from time to time. The first one in the water would get healed. Wow! How far from God's revelation of himself had these people fallen. How desperate were they to try anything?

Apparently, the truth is that the stirring was caused by an underground stream bubbling up from time to time and had nothing to do with angels. However, back to the question of what on earth were the people of God looking to some fable for healing rather than the Almighty himself, who had declared himself to be, Jehovah Rapha, the Lord your healer? (Ex 15:26) They should have known better. We'd never do that today would we?

I was shocked to learn that a poll in Italy showed that of the top ten people who prayed regularly, Jesus only got to number seven. Six other people are thought to be more likely to answer prayer than he is. Wow! I guess a lot of them would be around the pool at Bethesda. And here it is. The moment we slap a bit of religion over a load of nonsense and superstition and call it God. It's not just the Italians who do it, we all do. House of Grace or House of Disgrace?

When God is silent

It is true that the nation had not heard from God for four centuries, Malachi being the last recorded prophet to speak God's word. When we don't hear the voice of God it is a guarantee that we'll veer off track. Worse still we'll often do it whilst claiming some form of biblical or religious basis. You can see it all around with weird and wonderful ideas about life given the 'God' stamp. We explain our life through our current understanding and then try to add God to it. The less we hear from God the more likely that our starting place will be incorrect and, if that is wrong, you can be sure that our finishing place will also be way off. We end up explaining God from our viewpoint or culture rather than humbly 'trembling at his word.

God, as it turns out, doesn't think too highly of that approach. (Is 66:2)

The paralysed man

Thirty-Eight years is a very long time if you're waiting. We know for sure he was not a youngster, and we also know that he'd got into a life of sin. Jesus' closing statement to him, 'stop sinning or something worse may happen' (v14), was not the normal way he signed off healings. In contrast to the miracle in chapter 9 with the man born blind who went on to become a disciple of Jesus, this guy seems to have gone away.

Let's look at what on earth Jesus was doing at a place filled with superstitious people during a Passover celebration. The Passover beautifully reminded them that God is *their* powerful deliverer. Despite being faced by the most feared opposition in the known world at that time God came through and set his people free (Exodus 3-12 – it's a great read). Jesus takes time out from celebrating his Father's amazing deliverance for Israel to go to a superstitious water hole full of ill people.

The only recorded healing that Jesus did was this man but given that he didn't go there for the view there may well have been many others. It was time to remind the folk there that it was God who healed not some strange apparition. Jesus will always take your attention away from myths and fables back to who he is himself. Jesus is so often in the middle of our muddle and distress looking to heal. Isn't he great?

He starts questioning the guy with a funny notion, 'do you want to get well?' Well, of course, he does Jesus! Why else would he be here at Bethesda! Or did he?

Do you *want* to get well?

We live in one of the parts of the Alps that has very pure air. Consequently, we have a lot of clinics and centres for people with all sorts of respiratory problems. Now both my wife and I have had our fair share of medical issues over the years. We've consequently had numerous appointments at different hospitals and clinics around our region. One of the scariest things we see are the people who have become institutionalised, almost content with being ill. They are happy to stay as the focus of doctors, specialists and nurses. It's not all by any means but enough to make you so glad to get out of those places. 'Do you want to get well?' may be exactly the right question.

Sometimes life has ground us down and we no longer care or are too tired to get well. This often happens when we are in a life of sin. Just as Adam and Eve hid from God when they sinned, so the instinct remains to hide behind illness or any excuse rather than face up to what is really going on. Ask it of yourself, do you want to get well, not just physically, but spiritually, emotionally, mentally and so on. Getting well can mean entering the scary world of loving others and all that it can cost. As Jesus so delicately put it, 'whoever wants to be my disciple, must deny themselves *(ouch)* take up their cross (*ooh no!)* and follow me *(to where?)*'. (Mt 16:24) So ask yourself again — do you want to get well? Ask until he answers.

Back to the story. The man describes the legend of the waters as though Jesus hadn't heard the story. Jesus didn't discuss the stupidity of such superstitions but simply demonstrated his Father, (this is the part where God blasts through the mumbo jumbo of life we create).

'Get up *(but I can't),* pick up your mat *(not allowed on the Sabbath!)* and walk *(impossible!)*' (v8).

The man did it. He was completely healed. God's words are not just another line of a book, they come with power. Jesus was not saying 'give it a try' but literally as the words were spoken the power came with it to make it happen.

I want to encourage you on this line. One day I was convinced God wanted me to marry my girlfriend, it did help that I was crazy about her as well, but I knew that God wanted to call me a 'husband'. Many times, and particularly when I've not been, shall we say, the ideal husband, I've reminded myself that God himself called me to be one. With that comes all the power I will need to be everything that God has called me to be as a partner to my wife.

It is the power of God's word that enables me, not me trying to do the best I can. One of the side effects of having a stroke is that your ability to control your emotions can go haywire. God said 'husband,' not 'husband until you have a stroke'. I could go on, but needless to say that the power of Jesus' words is so much more than information, they are life, if you want to get well. I had to fight for it, but it came.

The leaders and my Dad

The story doesn't end so well for this guy. He finds out that it was Jesus who healed him and goes off to the Jewish leaders to tell them (v15). Jesus ends up defending who he is, his ministry and then counters with attacking their total unbelief (v16-18). To them the rules they'd created were of greater importance than an astonishing healing. This is the section of the chapter where all the times the word believe are recorded.

The incredible statement of 'very truly I tell you, whoever *hears my word* and *believes him* who sent me *has* eternal life and will not be judged but *has* crossed over from death to life,' (v24), changed my dad's life. At 18, despite having been assured on many occasions that if he 'believed' that Jesus was the son of God he would be OK he still found no peace. In the end it was not human words that got him, but this simple verse and, in particular, the one word *'has'*. It was a done deal. It *had* happened, it was the *past* tense. It was not conditional on his behaviour or on what would happen in the future. It changed him. He says he was so excited he ran into the loos at his workplace and thanked God for the done deal. He went home (about a 40-minute bus ride) singing all the way. It must have been a sight, but he said he just couldn't stop. Out of that moment of God speaking, ten children have come (I'm number eight) who've followed Jesus. There are also 34 grandchildren and now great grandchildren. It was the power of the simple word '*has*' that opened this door …

Sadly, the leaders Jesus was addressing were so busy trying to find out what God wanted, that they missed it. In those days the Old Testament, as we know it, was widely studied by the religious. The Pharisee sect were on a mission to restore a wayward people back to the teachings of scripture and therefore back to God. They saw the Roman occupation as punishment for the faithless situation of the nation. It was their mission to put it right. So, who was this Jesus, blowing it all apart?

Notice the difference between the words 'study' and 'listen'. Jesus had said many times, 'he who has ears to *hear let him hear*,' (Mt 11:15; 13:9; Mk 4:9; Lk8:8). They thought they'd have eternal life by studying law, not by knowing a person. If we do that, then, like them, we won't be ecstatic with joy about an amazing healing, we'll just look for ways to try to shut it down.

I know of a church that had prayed for God to move in their town for many years. He did, but it was in the shape of unruly youngsters and ex-drug addicts. They were largely shunned by the community and, little surprise, the move petered out. Unbelievably sad.

I know miracles are not the only proof of how and why, but they are the most amazing attention grabbers. They should make us sit up and take notice even if we don't understand. Above all, they should make us listen.

Finally

In life it is often said if you want to find out the why you need to follow the money. I've found that 'following the fruit' for the follower of Jesus is the way of finding out where Jesus is in you and your group's life. Where are the miracles happening? Where are the fruits of the kingdom being displayed? Where is the bible being lived out? Here's where you'll find Jesus at work.

When we arrived in France a pastor friend from the UK said to us that 'what God was going to build here would be like nothing else we'd seen before.' My guide on 'how to do it' and my experience have had to give way to watching and listening.

Jesus included the Bible in this. '*You study the scriptures diligently because you think that in them you have eternal life. These are the very scriptures that testify about me, yet you refuse to come to me to have life.*' (v39, 40). He spoke to the religious leaders. Yet they were a million miles away.

You won't be studying the Bible when we're with Jesus in our new home. He is what it was all about. The reality will be there. Keep chasing the reality now. Yes, study the scriptures, God speaks loads to me through them, but remember the goal is a person, and that person wants to speak to you.

Asha's friend was on her last try for a baby. All previous attempts at becoming pregnant through IVF had failed and she was on her last remaining two eggs. Sadly, part way into the process she started bleeding, and she sent a text to Asha to pray as she was on her way to hospital. She is not a follower of Jesus. Asha got on her knees and immediately was overwhelmed with emotion. God gave her Psalm 113 and after wading through verses that didn't seem relevant, she came across verse 9, 'He settles the childless woman in her home as a happy mother of children'. She told her friend it would be alright, that God was going to give her a child. The friend was operated on and miraculously one of the eggs was saved. They met several weeks later in a supermarket where she showed off a very pregnant tummy. Asha told her all that God had said. They cried and hugged. Asha prayed; God spoke. A baby was saved.

We all need to be Stupid Boys!

John Chapter 6

You Stupid Boy!

Growing up one of our favourite family TV programmes was called *Dad's Army*. It was an easy-going comedy about a group of men who were unable to go and fight for their country in WW2 called the Home Guard (an actual historical group in the war). Their job was to stay home and protect the local area. One of the characters portrayed was the youngest member of the Warmington-on-Sea Home Guard, called Private Pike. He classically often said or did the wrong thing, eliciting the frequently repeated phrase from his commanding officer, the beleaguered Captain Manwaring, 'You Stupid Boy!' I've often thought that this phrase might have been aimed at Andrew in this chapter.

This chapter tells of one of the most spectacular miracles performed by Jesus, which is then followed by one of the seven great 'I am' statements in this gospel.

Feeding a lot of people

Feeding five thousand people might seem way, way out of our league. We're glad when God helps us find the keys we've misplaced or gives us a good night's sleep. Feeding five thousand hungry people with nothing? No. Yet still he asks Philip the question, 'How are we going to feed them?' (v5).

Faced with an impossible request we'd normally start as the disciple Philip did by the 'let's be sensible' comment.

'No way do we have enough money, and even *if* we did, the supermarket is too far away! (v7) Be reasonable Jesus!'

Bring on the Stupid Boy, Andrew.

Not a lot is known about Andrew. We know he was great at introducing people to Jesus. He was a follower of John the Baptist (John 1:35) and therefore hungry for more than he had. John's message was a preparing one and he pointed Andrew to Jesus. Andrew very quickly brought his brother Peter saying, 'we have found the Messiah,' (1:41). If that was all he did I think we'd all be incredibly grateful. What an amazing blessing Peter was to become and still is. Andrew was the key to Peter but it didn't stop there. We often quote Peter as being the first disciple to see the good news go outside the Jewish nation and Paul as the great apostle of the gentiles, but it was Andrew together with Philip who first brought Greeks to Jesus (Jn 12:20). He was eager to help!

Five thousand hungry men plus women and children are there. Note here that Jesus, '*already had in mind what he was going to do*' (v6). God always knows what he is going to do. He involves us because he wants us next to him. Take courage – he already has the answers.

The stupid comment becomes the miracle

'*Here is a boy with five loaves and two small fish*' Andrew says and, just in case you thought he was aware Jesus could multiply them, he adds, '*but how far will they go among so many?*' (v9).

Altogether: 'You Stupid Boy!'

I guess Peter would've liked to clip him round the head, as older brothers do. I'm sure the others were just bewildered that he'd even suggest that, given the enormity of the problem facing them. A small picnic. You Stupid Boy indeed!

Yet it was these very loaves and fishes that Jesus used to perform the great miracle and open the door to some life-changing teaching. Everyone ate their fill and each disciple managed to get a basket of leftovers for Ron (this is our family term for keeping food for later consumption without people knowing what you're up to: 'It's for Ron' = it's for me, later on).

Andrew's doing 'what he could' was enough.

Amazing isn't it, God isn't asking you to do things you can't, he just wants your loaves and fish. He'll do the impossible part. Often my wife and I start our day by offering God our loaves and fish and ask him to multiply them in the life we lead.

Andrew's offer was the catalyst moment that fed thousands. We all need to be Stupid Boys!

Being cool in the storm

The miracle didn't stop there. A long day had been capped with the disciples having to row across Lake Galilee through a very heavy storm without Jesus. They must have been exhausted after having fed all those people. Their 12 baskets were difficult to keep dry in the pounding waves in their little boat (v16-18).

Jesus suddenly appears walking on the water, (v19). (I did try it once as a young Christian. I just got wet.) He gets in the boat after calming them all down and gives them an instant ride that made Red Bull power boats look like rubber bath ducks (v20-21). Jesus knows how to look after his own. An instant transport that makes hyperspace speed look slow.

If this was a Hollywood production, the story would have been over. Thousands of people healed and fed by Jesus, topped off by walking on water and an instant ride. It would make a great movie. Yet Jesus is not that bothered about the miracles, he wants the people. He's frustrated that all they seem to care about are their own stomachs and their own problems (v26-27). They're not going after what's important in life.

Stop looking for miracles and start looking for the BREAD of LIFE

Do not be surprised that Jesus isn't only concerned with the problems you're facing. Your health, your finances and even your relationships are only the first steps, he wants us. This is the real miracle we need, Jesus at the heart of our life.

We can tolerate, perhaps even half understand when he says, '*I am the bread of life*' (v48). But when he says, '*unless you eat the flesh of the son of man and drink his blood, you have no life in you*' (v53), the first thought is revulsion. Even more so that he was teaching in a Jewish synagogue when he said it. Eating unpermitted foods was forbidden in the country and you never, but never drank blood. No Black Pudding here!

Does Jesus ever shock you when he speaks? Do we read something in the bible and think of why that might not apply to us today? Be careful. He is the same yesterday, today and forever (Hb 13:8). Like the audience here, there are parts of Jesus we just don't like, so we try to rub them out. It is quite convenient and not that hard to build a Jesus around our views of how the world should work. As Voltaire said, *'In the beginning God created man in his own image, and man has been trying to repay the favour ever since'.* We end up creating, yes and even worshipping, the God of our own creation.

If we do that, we're not listening nor are we 'knowing him'. He is an offence to the way our culture thinks, and not just the people that we like to disagree with. If you really want to hear him in your life and in the life of your group, *'eat his flesh and drink his blood.'* Yes, I know this is talking about his crucifixion and resurrection, but it is also Jesus shaking out people who only follow him for what they can get out of him. We won't take up our cross and follow Jesus if we only want our needs met.

When the crowd went, including many of his followers (I guess he didn't take the Instagram or Tik Tok tips to heart on how to increase your audience) he turned to his disciples and said, *'do you want to leave too?'* (v67.) Simon Peter turns and says one of the great statements you MUST keep central if you want to hear God in your life, (and thank you again Andrew for introducing him to Jesus,) *'Lord, to whom shall we go? You have the words of eternal life. We have come to believe and to know that you are Holy one of God*' (v68, 69).

When, despite all that is horrible and wrong in your life, you can join Peter and say those words, you're ready to hear with a new clarity.

I've come to find his words like a hot shower. I stand under it, even if it is a little painful, as I must get clean. First my wife, then my friends and finally everyone starts complaining if I don't. His word is a hot shower into your life, your relationships, your businesses all that is important.

Make sure you get in there every day, if not it will show.

A close friend of mine, when he was 18, was out on a walk talking to Jesus. He heard a voice saying, 'pastor my people'.

He went on to do ten jobs over his life including running four businesses, a church pastor, and several community projects. Over his years he's had twenty-five different cars, four dogs, three children, eight grandchildren, lived in three countries and still has a beautiful wife. Yet that one phrase has guided and focused every life decision he has made.

One phrase from God, and a life is shaped.

Who fills your tap?

John Chapter 7

Where Does the River Flow From?

We live at the head of one of the most beautiful valleys in France called La Vallée de la Clarée. The breath-taking mountain scenery is enhanced by a beautiful river that gives the valley its name, La Clarée. At our village it is joined by a little stream called the Durance. This little stream, that comes from the mountain pass behind us, changes the name of the river to the well-known river, La Durance.

La Durance travels down and goes into the largest manmade lake in Europe (until 2017 it was the largest in the world) and from there provides irrigation for one of France's great fruit growing areas. It makes electric power through a system of canals and hydro turbines, and supplies drinking water to hundreds of thousands of people. It also provides a great deal of fun on the lake itself.

When Jesus said, *'Let anyone who is thirsty come to me and drink, whoever believes in me, as the Scripture has said, rivers of living water will flow from within him'* (v37, 38), I often think of the little name changing stream that goes onto supply millions with food, power, life and joy.

Why the name change for our river? Surely the bigger river would get priority. It's thought it's because from the earliest record of the name (around 1st century) the Durance flowed from a place where there was an important and well-used route across the Alps. La Clarée, in contrast, flows from a cul-de-sac. As stunning as it might be, at the end of that valley there are no routes, just mountains.

So, here's the question, where does your river come from? What comes out of your group or your life that feeds, empowers and gives life?

Who fills your tap?

Jesus is clear to where his source is, it's his Father. When the people said of Jesus, '*where did he get such teaching seeing as he's never been taught?*' (v15), we hit upon a fundamental and hugely important principle of life. The reason Jesus kept on repeating the phrase '*Whoever BELIEVES in me*' is because the only source he had was his Father (v16). Therefore, if you *BELIEVED* in him, you were *BELIEVING* in the one who sent him. You were believing in the God of Israel, the creator, the source of all life.

The opposite was also true, if you reject Jesus or his teaching you also reject his Father. You couldn't have Jesus without the Father. When Jesus said 'My teaching is NOT my own. It comes from the one who sent me' (v16), it was because his whole goal was to connect people to his Father. He took great pains to make it clear that 'he ONLY did what he saw his Father doing. In chapter 5v19 he'd said he '*can do nothing by himself, he can only do what he saw his Father doing*'.

The other rivers of teaching originated from men, the cul-de-sac of their own ideas and discoveries. Many may be good, they may look very attractive, but they do not carry life that only Jesus can bring. Don't be tempted to think that there are good resources out there in the world for us. Jesus didn't. If he didn't, we mustn't. Yes, La Clarée is a very beautiful river, but it's not the river that brings life to millions. If you want to be more than just a pretty river that people admire, if you want to bring life to people, you must make sure that your source is God himself.

I have a friend who I love dearly. Every time they hear that someone's a Pastor or has gone to a Bible College, they go into an awe that drives me mad. Now, I have nothing against learning, but it's not a college or job title that gives you authority to speak or change the world around you. Our authority is that we learn to 'only do what you see the Father doing'. You may learn that at a college or not, the important thing is that you learn it. Jesus, for the record, never went to college.

Watch out, they're from a dodgy background!

Many of the people in this chapter just couldn't see it. They even had *proof* that Jesus, despite the amazing miracles he did, couldn't be true. The scriptures said he'd be born in Bethlehem and not from Galilee (v41,42, 52). Of course, they had not had to suffer eight years of nativity plays as I did when my children were in primary school. I knew beyond any shadow of doubt where Jesus was born. I also knew that the angel's wings occasionally fell off and that baby Jesus was frequently held in the most ungainly positions.

Here is a big warning. I know I'm jumping around chapters a little here, but this is the place to do it. Studying the Bible will get you no nearer the truth than studying your local newspaper. Shall I say it again? Studying the Bible will not get you any more answers than studying a tourist brochure.

How dare I say that? Well look at who Jesus' main opponents were here (v32). They were the spiritual leaders of their day, the people who interpreted 'the will of God' for the nation. These people, Jesus said, thought they could find eternal life by searching the scriptures (John 5v39). You really can't.

Am I saying don't read the Bible? Don't listen to spiritual leaders? Don't read books like this? Well, yes and no. If you do it without a conscious awareness of the Holy Spirit guiding and leading you (we'll catch more of this in Chapter 16) and making Jesus (who is the **point** of the Bible) real to you, you'll get nowhere. You'll just end up confused or worse, a religious bigot. You will not get to the promise Jesus gave in v37, rivers of living water flowing from your innermost being. You'll be as useless as an old bottle of wine that looks great on the label but has gone sour.

Millions of people around the world study the scriptures and they pray. Yet, how many start their day saying, 'Father what are you doing today? Show me more of you? Let me do what you're doing'. Another way of saying, your kingdom come, your will be done.

Let me balance it here as I'm not saying we don't need to dig into God's word. If we don't read the Bible, we never understand or know the God who has *chosen* to reveal himself in Scripture. It is one of the principal ways the Holy Spirit speaks, and we ignore it at our peril. Jesus himself quoted from 15 books, 78 times; he knew it back to front. Even the guards sent to arrest Jesus were so amazed by his teaching that they couldn't carry out their orders (v45-46).

Yet, still, it's the Holy Spirit who brings it to life.

It might well be that you put this book down and go for a long walk to be alone with him. It may be that in your group's 'worship' time you give more time to listen than just to sing. It may be that you stop copying the Bible and you start following Jesus (think about that one). I want to bring that river, not so people look at me, but that they start looking at Jesus.

Will it all look the same?

My grandson Max recently grabbed me and made me come and see the amazing construction he'd built with a well-known toy. This toy has been around for decades, and both his father and I had built great constructions with it in our childhoods. Each generation made something completely different. I had no idea of how Max's world worked until he patiently explained it to me. Yet, and here's the important yet, it was clear that the source material was the same. The only thing that will authenticate and make a difference to what you do is that your source material will be the same. The Father, the source of all life.

In my younger years when pennies were tight, we'd buy cheap furniture. They'd seem fine to begin with but would eventually break and end up costing more than a good quality item. They weren't fine and we now try never to do that. If we have a different source than Jesus, we'll put a weakness in our life that'll end up breaking.

Please don't go all religious on me, keep in mind the picture I gave of another grandson Boaz and his toy mower. Just keep your eye on Jesus, be simple, be honest, be talkative and above all, listen.

The Brothers

Ah yes, we can't leave this chapter without a mention of Jesus' brothers. They seem to have been goading Jesus into a dangerous situation. People were not just trying to debate with Jesus, some were trying to kill him. Yet still his younger brothers, who it says, '*did not believe in him*', wanted him to go up to Jerusalem (v1-5).

Two of the great joys I had as a youngster were not very nice. I had two older brothers living at home. The first was five years older and I made him cry once by tripping him onto a sharp corner of a wall. It must have been incredibly painful. Did I care? No! I'd made my brother cry. I had revenge for all the years of his domination, as he nursed his bleeding head. My other older brother, a mere four years my senior, was the personification of patience and gentleness. What was my crowning delight as a youngster? Rejoicing in his display of the fruits of the Spirit? Not a bit of it. I once, and I say it again, ONCE, made him lose his temper. Many times, my goal was to annoy him, as only a younger brother can, and once I got the reaction I was looking for.

You'll be glad to know that as I grew up, I've come to love and honour those two brothers dearly and respect and appreciate what they bring to life. I love it that James, the brother of Jesus, was one of the early church leaders and wrote a book about following him. Things move on. Be careful in your heart on how you think of 'successful' Christians, particularly those close to you. Are you jealous, critical, delighting in their problems? Then the 'problem' rests with you. Ask forgiveness and then find out from Jesus what you could do to be a blessing to that person.

JAMES HODSON

John was lying awake in his bed. He was asking God how he could communicate who Jesus was to his autistic son who didn't respond to language. At that moment his wife turned over in her sleep and put her arm around him. She normally needed her space to sleep so this never happened. John felt a deep healing over many things that had happened in the last years. He realised that, though not a single word had been spoken, so much had been imparted. God didn't need words to speak. His son was going to enjoy God as much as anyone.

Our dependency on each other in understanding the voice of God is our strength and our safety.

John Chapter 8

That's Your Opinion.

One of the great wet blankets put over people to stop them hearing God is that people say, 'it's only your opinion'. This happens particularly when you disagree with them, in which case you quickly become wrong, prejudiced, misguided and so on. Growing up I knew how to argue. Being number eight of a litter of ten, I think it was my special gift. Black could be white if I wanted, I didn't care as long as I won the argument. This ability to disregard fact for opinion has caught on in almost every area of our world. I suspect social media hasn't helped this but, in this chapter, Jesus seems to be dealing with the same problem.

When people talk about this chapter most go to the amazing story of the woman caught in adultery. Great questions like, where was the man? since you can't 'catch' someone in adultery on their own. What was Jesus drawing in the sand? What were the sins people were remembering? I've heard many great sermons on the subject and the phrase *'let him who is without sin cast the first stone'* is still used in common language today (v1-8). I'm going to take a different look at this chapter, the subject of arguing and personal opinions and how they can intimidate us from listening to God.

Well in my Opinion …

I sometimes wonder why so much of this quite amazing gospel has so many references to Jesus arguing with people. I'd get it if he was a politician or a Man Utd fan like me, but clearly not.

What is so important about recording people's opinion who think he was a foreigner, demon possessed, blasphemous, misguided and so on, to the point they wanted to kill him? (v59). Virtually the whole of this chapter is given to arguments, that is, apart from four great power statements. Firstly, when Jesus said to the woman caught in adultery, '*Woman where are they? Has no-one condemned you? Neither do I condemn you, go and leave your life of sin,*' (v10, 11). Secondly, '*I am the light of the world. Whoever follows me will never walk in darkness but will have the light of life,*' (v12). Thirdly, '*if you hold my teaching …then you will know the truth and the truth will set you free,*' (v32) and finally, '*if the Son sets you free you're free indeed,*' (v36).

Here's the rub, each of these amazing comments rather than leading people to worship, listen and follow seem to have elicited arguments as to why he was wrong! How depressing.

So where do we go?

I've never ceased to be amazed at one aspect of my relationship with little children. My daughter from when she could first speak seemed to have a great distrust of my abilities. It's carried onto the next generation where my grandchildren seem to have no worry about saying, 'not like that grandad'. It's not just my own offspring either. There is a weird mistrust of my capabilities that I seem to engender with little children. Do I give off an air of total incompetence? Or worse, am I totally inept and they are the only ones with the honesty to say it. (We all know the little child (me included) that will say, 'Mummy, why does that woman have a beard?') Perhaps I really shouldn't be trusted with anything important.

How do you move forward if you're listening to God but no-one else thinks that it's right, or even important. Have we as Christians grown weary of people who say, 'God said, God said,' and yet have lives that are negative and irrelevant to the world they are in? We start to shut our ears to it.

I've put together three checks to help us avoid swallowing everything we hear whilst really valuing the voice of God. This will take it out of the world of opinions and into the world of truly being led by the Spirit.

- **True words from God, put him at the centre.** Jesus argues that he can testify that he's telling the truth because, without putting too fine a point on it, he is God (v14-18). Does what you hear and what you bring 'from God' make Jesus big or not? Prophecies that make you the all-important one, are at best polluted and at worst quite deceptive. We only find out what to do, who we are, where we are going when it is centred on Jesus. We find our place as we find the will of God (Col 1:9-12) and he is bringing all things under his son, Jesus. That's the gameplan. Don't settle for another. (v54; Ep 1:22; Rev 11:15.)

- **Does it have witnesses? We're part of a body.** Is it just you or does anyone else think 'yeah, I'm getting it'. Jesus said that he and his father made up the two witnesses (v18) demanded by the Jewish law. I'm not a great dreamer. My wife assures me that 'young men will see visions, and old men will have dreams' (Joel 2:28) and that therefore I should have moved into the 'dream' world and away from 'visions'. Some of my dreams have turned out to be alarmingly accurate and have unlocked impossible situations. Others probably had more to do with the cheese fondue I'd had the night before and little else. I'm not bothered. 'Whoever belongs to God, hears what God says,' (v47) is a huge comfort. My church family, my friends have been great witnesses as to whether it's God speaking or the fondue.

- **Did it work? Follow the fruit ...** In Isaiah God said this, *'my word that goes out from my mouth: It will not return to me empty but will accomplish what I desire and achieve the purpose for which I sent it,'* (Is55:11). Wow, powerful! When Jesus said in this chapter, *'I am the light of the world. Whoever follows me will never walk in darkness but have the light of life.'* (v12), millions, including me, have found it to be true. When I started to follow Jesus, light came into my life, showing the right path and exposing less helpful areas at the same time giving me the grace to adjust course (a job still in process until I leave this world!). I have prophesied all kinds of things to all sorts of people during my life. Some of them have been quite big and in front of crowds, some in a quiet moment. How do I know if they were right or not? They usually happen. If they did not, I apologised. Humility is not an enemy. It keeps us where we should be, dependent on Jesus.

To finish up ...

One of the reasons some of us get so worked up about whether it was God speaking or not, is that we hate being wrong. Our world falls apart and we're humiliated. I suspect human pride is right up there as the cause of this reaction. We humans are, according to studies, very good at overestimating our abilities, highlighting the good and burying the bad. The Jewish religious leaders had spent years perfecting an understanding of God and his law, only for Jesus to drive a bulldozer through it. No wonder they kicked up. No wonder we do the same.

Can I remind you of Balaam's donkey who spoke to the prophet (Nu 22:21-39). If you speak God's word, you're currently on a level with a donkey. Don't get stressed, you're only being an 'unworthy servant' as Jesus wisely put it (Lk 17:10).

God has designed us as a body, and we can only function if we're being a body. Therefore, know in your innermost being that you NEED other people in your Christian family to fully understand God's voice. Our basic design is as a body, (1 Co 12 has a full explanation,) so unless we act in our lives as part of one, we are going to get it wrong. There is no place for 'the independent thinker,' so vaunted in our western culture.

Our humble dependency on each other in understanding the voice of God is our strength and our safety.

As we pursue the life-giving words of Jesus together, we'll find the will of God and the path he has for us.

Ben had had a rough run. Tough business situations year after year had left him feeling beaten up. The story of Joseph in the bible had really struck a note and he strongly felt that the role of keeping his world alive in a famine was a role God was speaking to him about. He didn't know why but he was sure God was talking.

Covid struck. It devastated the tourist sector, the business world he was involved in. But God had already given Ben the playbook.

God was true to his word and there was 'always enough' resource not just to keep everyone in their jobs, but also to pay all the businesses and people who relied on his company.

Not only had God spoken, but his words had given life to many.

We're in this world not primarily to make it a better place but to do his will.

John Chapter 9
Mud Pies are Hard Work

Our children loved making mud pies when they were little. The grubby hands, the dirty clothes and the inevitable washing piles were not their concern. They'd clearly already seen the adverts that claimed dirt was easily dealt with by the latest cleaning product, so why should they worry? That was their parents' job.

Waiting for the right moment

The miracle that Jesus performs here is very unusual. He was also making mud pies. Why? Well, I've heard differing theories on this, and you'll be glad to know I'm not going to add my own except I love that it shows that God doesn't mind getting his hands dirty. No, today I want to emphasise the strangeness of this miracle. So strange that above all else it teaches us *NOT* to follow formulas but to listen for the leading of the Holy Spirit.

Mud pie making isn't in any manual that I've ever seen. I've been trained on many 'how to' sessions in my life ranging from being a pastor, a husband, a father, evangelism and almost any Christian topic you'd care to mention. Yes, you can take useful stuff from the sessions (like try listening to your wife for once!) but it can and must never replace the immediacy of listening to the Holy Spirit in a situation. I've learnt in difficult moments as husband and wife where we can't seem to agree on a subject that to ask the advice of the Holy Spirit on the spot reaps huge rewards. The leading of God at that moment frequently involves the word 'sorry' on my part (I know bizarre, isn't it?) but it has so often resolved the disagreement and given us a positive way forward.

I love the word of God and I love pastoring people. Though not an evangelist, these passions spill out all the time to people who don't yet know Him. How do I get ready for these moments? For sure, I 'stock up' on the word of God and what it says about him and his incredible news. However, I've also come to *expect* that Jesus will want to do something different in whatever situation I'm in, so I've learnt to always ask him 'what should I do here?'

He is the one who says, 'him' or 'her,' or 'do this' or 'do that,' or frequently, 'just love them' or 'say nothing'. This doesn't mean that I can be weird in these moments, like in some kind of trance, it's that I need one ear constantly open. I'll throw up the prayer, 'Lord, is there anything you want me to do here?' After all, I'm his servant, and that's what servants do.

Hearing it right

My middle child Josh was a delight but sometimes he didn't always follow the guidelines precisely. He was around eight years old and had been the subject of some pretty intensive bullying at school. Despite several visits to the teachers, this hadn't stopped so I undertook to give him some self-defence training one weekend. We couldn't just let his school life be dominated by bullies, could we? Don't get me wrong I'm not a martial arts freak, it was basic stuff. The training was enough, I hoped, to stop the nonsense. On the day of his return to school, my wife got a call that we should go and see the headmaster.

'Ah! At last, a stop to the bullying,' I thought, 'good news.'

Well, yes and no. The bullying had stopped that day but not quite how we'd expected. Apparently, our son had walked into school, straight up to the tormentor and flattened him with an almighty punch.

'This sort of behaviour is not acceptable,' the headmaster boomed.

'Nor was the bullying,' I replied irritated at his one-sided approach, 'and yet nothing was done to stop it.'

A secret pleasure followed mixed with confusion. He *had* stood up for himself, but *I know* we hadn't told him to do *that*. The bully never harassed him again.

If we don't hear Jesus properly, we may well do some of what he said but we'll also miss it. Maybe we'd have just made mud pies; perhaps just sent the man off to the pool at Siloam. If God wants to use us to open up a situation, we'll need to know the what, when and how.

Listening and obeying is not only crucial, but it gives a confidence to his followers that he's there, right in the heart of the situation. The good news is that his ways are the right ones and even things that are unclear are that way for a reason. We'll get to that in the next chapter.

The Response

The Bible is peppered with the importance of pleasing God rather than people, and it occurs in John four times (5:30, 44; 8:29; 12:43). Jesus was not looking for man's approval, but his Father's. In our marriage we've found that the harder we work at pleasing God, the better our life together is. He is the true source of the joy and peace we all crave.

Just look at the reaction to this outstanding miracle. Here was a man who had never seen the light of day. He was physically blind in a culture where people were sure that his problem was either his sin or his parents (aren't we crazy when we go down these rabbit holes?). The man had been reduced to begging (v8) and there was nothing for him to look forward to.

The miracle itself was not like any other we read of in the gospels. The making mud pies with spit, putting it on his eyes, still blind yet going off to a pool to wash (I hope he had friends), and only then, wonder of wonders, complete clear 20/20 vision. I've seen people healed of cancer, of deformities and other impossible illnesses but I have never seen someone born blind healed. Wow!

This healing happened on a Sabbath. Of course, it did. Why would God want to do it on another day when he could annoy the religious. Why not press home his kingdom on a Thursday? I'd have done it then so as not to create a problem but not the Father, oh no. 'Seconds out, round 9!' as they say in the boxing world, God was going for something bigger than just this healing, as powerful as it was. He had two other objectives I can see.

Is your mind right?

Religious opinion was divided. Some knew that Jesus could not possibly be from God because he broke the Sabbath rules (v16). Others saw the enormity of this healing and realised only God could have done this (v16). Be careful that your 'rules' of what you understand about God and life do not rule out Jesus when he comes by. It's a sad reality that often the latest works of God in a place are most fiercely resisted by other Christians..

When you and your group see, do and experience the amazing, do not think everyone will be delighted with you. Do not think that they will all start to follow Jesus as a result. For some you'll really get on their nerves, particularly the religious people. This part is quite hard to accept but as God's family we're in the world not just to make it a better place but we're here to do his will (5:19; 6:38). God divides (Mt 10:34-35). Miracles are a sign. The very ones you do will be a call to some to believe and follow. For others it will just be a witness that they did not hear when God came knocking. We don't get to decide on these things, that's God's job alone but nonetheless it's true. It is why it is so important to do what he says.

The Healed Man on a mission

We don't know exactly what happened to this man who was healed. We know that Jesus heard (v35) about him defending his healer when even his parent's bottled it. We know he really irritated the Pharisees, and was kicked out, not just of that meeting but out of the synagogue permanently (v22).

However, the most important thing we know is that Jesus found him and told him who the Son of Man was (v35-37). The man became a worshipper (v38) and given that the Pool of Siloam means 'Pool of the Sent', the obedience he demonstrated to get his healing, and the courage he showed in front of the authorities, my guess is he'd been picked by God to be a powerful sharer of the good news about Jesus.

We don't know why Jesus does things the way he does, but we know that he said, '*I* will build *my* church', (Mat 16:18). We *must* let him do it his way, no matter how bizarre it can seem. For that we need to be listeners, yes, even if mud pies are involved.

Next chapter we'll see how this is not just a possibility but is your birth right as a follower of Jesus..

Ariel was five. It was her auntie's birthday. She wanted to make a card for her as she loves drawing. God told her to do an apple tree.

The birthday card was sent. When her auntie received it, she phoned, and exclaimed excitedly, 'that's amazing, we've just planted 12 apple trees!'

Ariel knew that day. God wanted to use her art to speak to people. She's still only a child but many pieces of her art have already gone out.

We might believe but has that led to following?

John Chapter 10
That's *My* Shepherd's Voice

Here we get to the middle of this amazing book, and perhaps to the heart of the message of listening.

Daisy

I've developed some simple commands for our dog Daisy. A whistle from a long way off whilst she's playing with other dogs in the village will bring her back home. My son's dog, Rocky, a Malamute, will often come lumbering behind her. Maybe he also recognises the authority I carry or, more probably, he knows the likelihood of a dog biscuit is high. Either way they recognise my voice and come. The other dogs carry on playing. They don't recognise me, nor do they care.

What is it about my whistle that gets Daisy scampering home? She *knows* it's me. She is our dog. We bought her and placed her in our home. We feed, walk, pet and play with her. I've seen Daisy when strangers call her, she doesn't recognise them. Maybe she'll go over to see them if she thinks there's a game of ball to be had but otherwise, they mean very little to her. She knows other people in the pack, other family members and long-term friends and she'll go and say hi with her little waggy tail beating ferociously, however Daisy is our dog. She knows where her home is.

Hearing your Name

This 'whistle' is the essence of you being able to hear the voice of God in *your* life. You are his (V29), given to **Him** by the Father. When you were 'dead in your sins' **HE** made you alive, it was not *your* doing (Eph 2:5). He bought you and has placed you in *his* family. He feeds you; he exercises you (remember those not-so-easy days? That's him exercising us), he plays with you, and he loves you like no-one else ever can or will. You're 100 percent his.

Yes, you'll know others in the 'pack', you'll often recognise something about them, and you'll greet them with your tail wagging ferociously. I often cry the first time I hear people worshipping God from another country. My heart beats, 'they have the same owner, I sense it'. Every tribe, tongue and nation will have *his* sheep in them! The voice of a stranger won't have the same effect on you.

Listen out for the Whistle. Daisy always seems to have one ear cocked so that when we whistle, she'll come. Keep your ears open to his voice, He designed you to hear it. Here is your home.

Why do we not hear?

'All well and good', you say, 'but I don't seem to hear it, at least not that I'd know.'

The word *believe* is so crucial in this process. It's used 85 times in the gospel of John and is not just some quick throwaway term that has little importance. It is the central most important thing that will enable you to hear his voice clearly. Daisy does not go religious on me when I whistle. She might be irritated at having to stop a game or she might be eager at the thought that we're going to do something more fun; it doesn't matter, it's just natural. She just *believes* in me, and that belief sparks a faith that obeys. *Believe* that Jesus speaking to you is just a natural part of your daily life and not some strange religious experience that you set up a shrine to.

It's so important to understand that Jesus is *our* good shepherd and that we *can hear* his voice. This is not a theory. It is like when you're called for a meal. You believe, therefore, you head to the table and sit down. You believe the call and have faith that you're going to eat if you come. It makes you act. Yum!

You'll recognise it's Jesus. As much as he knows you, you'll know him (v14). Yes, those around you who don't yet know him, will think you're off your head, ready to be carted off to the nearest psychiatric hospital (v20) but it remains true, the follower of Jesus **can** hear his voice.

So, what stops us from being confident in hearing his voice? Here are five thoughts:

1. **We get frightened off by people thinking we're crazy**. This can come from inside and outside his family. We try to play it safe. We try to say the minimum about the Holy Spirit talking to us, so we're not thought too mad. Be sensible, be reasonable, don't appear too crazy! In this chapter Jesus claimed he was able to give '*eternal life*' (v28), that He and His Father (God) were one (v30). He said that he was 'in' the Father and the

Father was 'in' Him (v38). Crazy? Blasphemous? He clearly did not shy away from it, nor should we.

2. **We're too busy to listen**. We crowd our lives with so much we give no time to listen. This is a huge problem in a social media driven world where even sitting on the loo for two minutes can involve you in multiple discussions with situations and people everywhere. (I do admit to making the mistake of putting a call accidently on video whilst on the loo.) Practice some silent time each day. Put your phone away, go for a walk, lie on your bed and be quiet; whatever it takes to make the space.

3. **We're frightened we'll get it wrong.** Do it with others (see previous chapter). Jesus called out his sheep '**by name'** but he led '**them**' out (v3). Yes, you'll have your moment when you hear your name (it still blows me away) but the other sheep around you should be hearing their name and heading in the same direction. There's one flock and one shepherd (v16). There won't be a choice of thrones in heaven to gather around in worship! Yes, God has callings for many of us that take us to different situations, but it's one voice that we're all responding to.

If you're in a situation where you are standing alone, maybe you're not in *your* part of the flock. You are a 'living stone' being built into a spiritual house (1 Pt 2:5) and you need to be fitted with the stones around you. I've built stone walls in my garden. It takes time, but it's so much stronger and more interesting than bricks.

Ask Jesus to put you in the place where you'll fit. Look out for it. That doesn't mean that you'll always agree, not at all. You'll just recognise that this is home, this is my family. When I was 18, I walked into a church meeting I'd never been to before. I knew that this was the home God had prepared for me for that stage of my life. These were the people I could learn to hear his voice without worry. Many times, I got it wrong, increasingly I got it right. I learnt to recognise him.

4. **We've been hurt by people who claim to be speaking on behalf of God**. The crucial thing here is 'my sheep hear *my* voice'. It's right to test when someone tells you that they are speaking from God (including this book). Many people claim to be speaking on behalf of God, and some of them are nothing more than thieves or robbers (v1). They are more interested in power, control and personal glory than they are of sheep growing up to know Jesus. I prophecy a lot so I know the temptations of this. Three tips:

    1. Watch the fruit of that person's life. If you can't see it be careful (v12 & 25).

    2. Check that what they say ties in with God's word. It is like a plumbline that keeps us safe (v35).

3. Ask do they care about the people they are 'prophesying' to or are they a 'hired hand' (v11, 13).

5. **We're not yet 'his' sheep** (v26). We might 'believe' but has that led to following? A vague acknowledgement of God does not make you one of his sheep. It involves, as it did with his disciples here, leaving *everything* to follow (Mt 19:27). It's an attitude of heart, to be ready to do anything that he asks. That's following. It's the *sheep* that hears his voice.

If you're not sure, pray right now 'Lord, I want to be one of *your* sheep, I want you to lead me'.

So, finally, what good does listening do?

What happens to the sheep who listen in this chapter? Five fantastic promises:

- they follow Jesus who goes before them (v4).

- they find good food to eat (v9).

- they are kept safe (v2, 3).

- they're given abundant life, and that for eternity (v10, 28).

- they receive a shepherd who'll give his life for them (v13, 15).

Finally

Just a last thought, don't forget not everyone thought Jesus was demon possessed because they argued how could someone so troubled do such wonderful things. Let's make sure we're doing 'wonderful' things as it beckons to those who God is calling and makes Jesus look good. Make sure we're a blessing in the place he's put us.

JAMES HODSON

Davey and Asha were enjoying an around the world trip. It had been an eventful as well as enjoyable time.

They were about to embark on the last leg of the journey, a five-week stay in Jamaica, when God said to them. 'Go back home.'

They did as he told them. A few weeks later Asha's father, who ran the small family business with his wife, was struck down with a stroke. It was a serious problem as many people had booked holidays through the company and the ensuing mess would have been huge.

Davey immediately knew why God had called him back. He took on everything and though he and Asha have moved on, the company still flourishes to this day.

When we listen first rather than act, we won't always do the obvious thing.

John Chapter 11

Listening can mean doing nothing.

My son Ben loves to go up to the top of a mountain and seemingly do nothing. He'll leave his bed at 02:30, climb to the top of one of our local mountains and just sit and wait with Rocky, his faithful dog. He can wait a long time.

Eventually, from the cold icy darkness comes a crack of light and his camera comes out. He will then take some of the most breath-taking photos of dawn over our local range you'll ever see. I don't like waiting, never have. I'd be more likely on my way to the local café tucking into a coffee and croissant than waiting up a mountain. Consequently, my personal stock of dawn photos over the Alps is zero and so I resort to stealing his.

God sometimes says wait when we'd rather be getting on and doing something. He's waiting for that crucial moment. We don't get it.

In this chapter Jesus listened carefully to his father and it meant doing nothing (v6) even though a close friend lay dying. And, yes, the friend Lazarus did die. It puzzled and frustrated all sorts of people like his disciples and the local friends who'd seen him do many miracles. It broke the sisters of the dead man.

Three Words

Three words was all it took in the end, 'Lazarus come out' (v43). Lazarus got up and was helped by people getting his grave bandages off, picked up on his old life as it was before. I say, 'as it was before' but I suspect he was never the same.

Four days into death and your body starts the autolysis process. Discolouration of skin, the bloating caused by the initial decomposition collapses and fluids are released from the body. It's why we get to smell so bad. Martha, the sister knew (v38).

Around a grieving and puzzling situation, where we would have cried as Martha, a sister, did '*if you'd been here, my brother would not have died*' (v21), some amazing things happened.

Jesus had said, '*this sickness will not end in death. No, it is for God's glory so that the Son may be glorified through it*' (v4) and boy was he right. Let's look at some of them:

- The disciples became ready to follow Jesus anywhere (v8,16).

- The disciples learnt just how important it was to obey God rather than be dominated by fear or another agenda (v8,9,10).

- Jesus got to say, '*I am the resurrection and the life. The one who believes in me will live, even though they die; 26 and whoever lives by believing in me will never die. Do you believe this?*"

(v25,26). A verse which has helped millions through the centuries.

- An incredible miracle was performed that caused a great many people to believe in him. (v45 and into 12:9-11).

How on earth God managed to put back together a decomposing body I have no idea. I guess he must be **all** powerful!

Listen before doing

All this came about because Jesus listened. When we listen first rather than act, we won't always do the obvious thing. We may seem to make the situation worse and may be criticised for doing it like we do. Although difficult sometimes, nothing is the best course of action. With God, the results are so worth waiting for. I've seen it so many times in my life.

My young nephew cried out, 'patience is rubbish,' when he'd been told he'd have to wait until he could open the presents. 'Just be patient,' the mother had said, eliciting the now famous cry. He was right, of course. Patience, although highly prized throughout scripture, is one of the harder ones to get used to. It goes to the heart of who you really trust and to why you do the things you do. From God's point of view, it's an excellent training tool for getting us closer to him.

We pray and listen more. We learn to act on God's command even if it hits our reputation. We learn that, in the end, he's the one in control of our lives and our situations.

If a heart is closed to God

I'm staggered by this miracle. If you ever wanted proof that God was bigger than any problem we could come up with, this was it. However, I'm even more astonished by the heart that says in response to this miracle, 'oh no! Now we'll have to kill Lazarus too!' (v53; 12:10).

Who were the people opposing Jesus? They were people, trying to negotiate a difficult path of keeping the Jewish traditions alive whilst not falling foul of the Romans (v48). They thought they were helping preserve their nation. In the end, they did. If they had not been so unbelievably blind as to try to kill the man who'd done such amazing miracles, Jesus would never have been crucified and you and I wouldn't be standing here today as forgiven people.

Even the High Priest couldn't help but prophesy, '*it is better for you that one man dies for the people than that the whole nation perish*' (v50, 51). We can't expect that God's great works will please everyone but don't let it stop you waiting, listening and then doing. '*A great many people will come to him*' if we do (v45).

Even the most violent opposition God uses for his purposes. I know that doesn't excuse us for our actions, but it does show that nothing, yes nothing, can thwart God (Job 42:2).

This should be a great encouragement as we follow Jesus where he leads and do the things he said. Yes, it might cost us our very lives, but even the hardness of people does nothing to stop God. I love the fact we read in the next book in the Bible, that many priests became obedient to the faith (Acts 6:7). Some of the most hardened opponents become disciples.

Josh had just moved to Switzerland as a 19-year-old to live. His local language knowledge was zero. At a conference he was invited by the leaders to come up on stage and share anything he felt God was giving him.

He did, in beautiful English, of course. The audience started to laugh. With no idea of what had gone on before, he found out that he'd given the exact same word as a lady had done in German just before him, even down to the expressions.

A man sitting in the audience later confided that although the woman's word had spoken to him, he was not sure it was from God.

What Josh listened to and shared sealed the deal.

Whatever I say is just what the Father has told me to say (v50).

John Chapter 12

Worlds apart

This chapter is one of those that brings a sword down on the human population. In another account of Jesus' life Matthew records him as saying, '*Do not suppose that I have come to bring peace to the earth. I did not come to bring peace, but a sword*' (Mt 10:34). Here we can see it in blinding reality. There is a message going out to all the world, but Jesus is clear in verse 48 that the very words he spoke would be used to condemn people who refused to believe. This goes against our nature.

My Dad was quite open when he didn't agree with someone and let us all know about it. I don't know what it was, but it made my mother always want to justify the culprit. Even if it was shown beyond all shadow of doubt that they'd indeed committed a crime, she would come out with a phrase that has lingered in our family through to the next generations … 'but they have many other good points'. You have to say this in a German accent (her native country) to get the full effect.

She meant it as a justification for whoever was there, her children, me included, generally used it as a back-handed compliment. If my sister had done something I deemed to be stupid, I would gleefully let her know by declaring 'don't worry you have many other good points!' Ouch!

Jesus was not saying that here. The very words that brought eternal life to some (v50) bring the final condemnation to others (v48).

In a way my Mum was right to believe the best in everyone. Jesus said he was not going to judge, that was left to God (v48). However, the important thing for us to note was that he just spoke out that which his father told him to say (v49).

Our job, if you like, is to throw the seed out as far and wide as we can. We bring the kingdom of God into as many situations as we can. It is God's job alone to judge how it's received, not ours.

Jesus' Friends

Here was Jesus enjoying a meal with friends. There are few things better in life. Out of the blue comes Mary, who'd been most upset about Jesus letting her brother die (11:32), pouring out what was, probably, the most expensive thing she owned. Nard was one of the most expensive products of its day. It originated in India and had to undergo a lengthy and costly process to become a perfume. It represented about a year's income for a worker and was usually saved for a very special occasion like a marriage.

Today's special occasion was the man who not only brought her brother back from the dead, but helped her finally understand that he was the Son of God who loved her and would give himself for her.

He, not the expensive perfume, was her most valued thing in life.

A perfume usually destined for the heads of dignitaries and kings was poured onto tired well-used feet. Her hair, which was a woman's glory in those days, was used to wipe the feet.

This isn't just valuing; it is humility before greatness. Here she was giving her most prized possession and using her personal glory to honour the man she loved.

And this is the point

This was the action Jesus was working into his followers. Did he need praise? Not a bit of it, but, as he says later, when you give up your life to follow him, you've found it.

What does that mean? I've found this quote helpful from the 'Desiring God' website of John Piper (https://www.desiringgod.org/articles/how-to-hate-your-life).

If men speak well of you, it doesn't matter much.
If they hate you, it doesn't matter much.
If you have a lot of things, it doesn't matter much.
If you have little, it doesn't matter much.
If you are persecuted or lied about, it doesn't matter much.
If you are famous or unheard of, it doesn't matter much.
If you have died with Christ, these things just don't matter much.

If you've not got to this place, then hearing God's voice will have little impact. Listening comes into its own when you've learnt to die (v24-26). This is what he meant by saying '*he who has ears to hear, let him hear*'. It is a daily exercise for sure, but it's so worthwhile (Lk9:23).

The Cheering Crowds

This crowd is different from the one at the feeding of the five thousand. There was no tangible benefit to them except Jesus had just done an unheard-of miracle in their neighbourhood. These were not the stories of years gone by, of prophets who'd raised the dead, this was happening here and now. So the cry goes out *'Hosanna, blessed is he who comes in the name of the Lord!'* (v13). This was a cry of praise and prayer, one that was used to welcome their predicted Messiah. He was really here; he's come at last!

Even the leaders of the day said, 'the whole world is going over to them' (v19). Something special was happening. However, it does contrast with only a hundred and twenty people praying in the upper room, waiting for the promised Holy Spirit (Ac 1:15).

Now I'm sure that many in this crowd went on to become followers of Jesus. Having lived through life, I also sadly know that not all would have done so. Maybe some in the crowd a few days later were also shouting, 'crucify him' (19:15). The crowd can be a dangerous measure of where our heart is. Singing at the top of your voice at a football match does not mean I'll give my life for my club. It might *feel* like that at the time. The feeling soon gives way to the 101 other things I'm doing.

Following Jesus is so much more than cheering for him. Don't get me wrong, I love being in huge crowds where thousands of people are singing and celebrating Jesus. However, it's not our goal. The goal is *'whoever serves me must follow me; and where I am, my servant will also be'* (v26).

We listen to Jesus and share his words, so that people will be *followers* of *him*. The crowd feeling we get on a Sunday night, doesn't always produce this on a Monday morning.

The Sword

When the non-Jews come to Jesus (again Andrew is involved) it's like Jesus could see just how far this gospel would go, and how important it was for him to lay down his life (v24,27). In turn, we as his followers, learn to '*hate their life in this world*' (v25,26). Our giving up of everything important to us, even to our very lives, is the means by which we '*enter eternal life'* (v25).

My parents-in-law had an old hand pump in their garden. You could get water out of it by vigorously pumping the handle, but it only worked if you were prepared to pour a measure of water down into the pump opening, called the prime, to start it off. I imagine on hot summer days when water was scarce it would be quite painful pouring down good clean water into the top of this pump. Yet if you didn't, you'd get no water back out. That's what it's like with our lives. We're priming the pump to give the water of life to many, including ourselves.

When God's voice boomed out his love and approval of his son (v28,29), it's worth noting how many of the people missed what was happening. It was either thunder or some other apparition to them. They were not listening for God.

Jesus deliberately sets out to frustrate the wisdom of this world, choosing *foolish* things over and above them to prove his point (1 Cor 1:19-29). Yet all is not lost, I love that even amongst 'the leaders' many started to believe in Jesus (v42).

Finally

Seven times again in this chapter, the word believe comes. This belief is like the sunrise. You know that amazing moment when all that was dark becomes plain and obvious and, in our mountains, above all beautiful (v46). It is the forerunner to listening and doing what he tells you, (v49). This in turn is what leads to eternal life (v50), not just for us but for so many more.

Like the gambler who puts all his money on one horse, put your whole life and being onto Jesus. Why? Because unlike the gambler, we know Jesus has already won.

God speaks to Ben through movies, amongst other things. The film Gladiator really struck him one day. Not the great battle scenes or the fight with the emperor which we might all know, but just how he organised broken and dispirited people into finding their place together and becoming an unstoppable force.

God was speaking to him about his life's role and his work. He was to bring people into their correct positions and enable them to achieve what they had been created to do.

He and his wife named their son Max so that this powerful lesson would never be far from them. A favourite phrase of his to this day is from the film, 'what we do in life, echoes in eternity'.

It is his pleasure to wash your feet.

John Chapter 13
The devil speaks too

The Father of lies

There has been a meteoric rise in the amount of disinformation around us. Politics, global pandemics, the environment and so on, there are people who set about to deliberately give out false information and, in doing so, try to destroy the reputation of others along with information that is reliable. Yuck, it's horrible. At the same time, the desire for fact and truth seems to have disappeared in favour of opinion. This isn't confined to the world we live in but has crept into the church. Double yuck!

Is this a new phenomenon? Maybe the extent of it is, but it's as old as the history of this planet. The first recorded disinformation and slandering of someone else's character appears in Genesis chapter 3. Here the devil openly challenges what God explicitly said to Adam and Eve. He then went on to bad mouth the character of God (Gen 3:1-6). He sowed the idea to them that God, far from being a kind, generous and loving person, was in fact, lying and trying to keep you away from good things. They had a choice to believe God or the serpent. They chose the serpent. And before we all pick up our pitchforks and clubs and go on a hunt to bash Adam and Eve, it's humbling to know that we've all done the same. I know I have.

I love the line of the Stuart Townend song 'How Deep the Father's Love' that says:

'it was my sin that held him there until it was accomplished'.

(Capitol Christian Music Group 1995)

In this chapter we see a man who chose to listen to Satan (v2) rather than the author of life he'd travelled with for three years. He's witnessed all the amazing miracles, heard all the life changing teaching. He'd even been part of the group of twelve (Mk6:7) and the seventy-two (Luke 10:1) sent out to heal the sick and cast out demons and tell everyone about Jesus. He'd known the very authority of God flowing through him (and if that doesn't tell us how our gifts from God are not because of our good character I don't know what will!). Finally, he even gets our Lord Jesus, the son of God and Son of Man, washing his feet. Yet still he has hidden something in his heart, and it allows him to listen to another voice.

How can Satan's voice come into *my* life?

We get our first clue in chapter 12:6 where we learn that Judas used to steal the money given to Jesus. It was given to him for his needs and for distributing to the poor (one of the lesser talked about aspects of Jesus' ministry was his financial aid charity). Why did he look after the purse? We don't know and aren't told. But it is clear that the temptation of money was big in his life. Maybe he volunteered to be the treasurer. Maybe he thought as many did that the Messiah was going to bring in a world conquering kingdom and he'd be right there as chief treasurer and doing very nicely thank you. Maybe he was worried about all the recent predictions Jesus had made about his death that he clearly wasn't going to become rich. Whatever it was there were warnings about betrayal (6:64; 6:71; 12:4) and there were many teachings on wealth and money (there are many references but maybe the two key ones are Mt 6:24; Lk 3:14) that Judas never followed in this area of his life. It was this very area that made him make a deal with the religious leaders, who valued Jesus with the same price paid for a slave (Ex 21:32).

I feel just a little scared.

I'm scared because I see just how corrupt humanity can be without God. Despite all the things Judas saw, experienced and tasted he was still corrupt in his core.

I also have a fear of a God who not only knew that this would happen, (it was prophesied in Psalm 41:9 and quoted in v18) but he used it to fulfil his own unstoppable purpose. Wow! even our sinfulness he'll use for his goals.

We should all be a little awed at this. But do we stay here? No, and the chapter gives some great ways where we can move forward because Judas is not the only character at play here.

Peter also messes up but ...

Firstly, here's how to get it wrong but get it right. Peter, thinking that he'll defend Jesus' honour to the death, is told like Judas that it's all going to go horribly wrong for him (v37,38). His arrogance and pride were about to be dealt a blow that would enable him to go on to become one of the main pillars of the church. The big difference is perhaps revealed in two words which are of great help.

In v36 and v37 Peter refers to Jesus as 'Lord'. He has had a revelation that Jesus is the Christ, the son of the living God (Mt 16:16). Despite all his mess ups, Jesus is *his* Lord. The last recorded statement of Judas Iscariot however refers to Jesus as 'rabbi,' (Mt 26:25) a term of honour for sure, but not God. Jesus never became Judas' God. Big failure.

Is Jesus your Lord? Does he have full right to all that you are, all that you have? For Peter, whose mistake prepared him for his mission, getting this right meant life. For Judas, who never got it, it was the end.

Letting Jesus wash *your* feet

A good friend of mine, Bernard Sanders, said that he starts each day letting Jesus wash him. He's involved in numerous projects around the world and many people quote his clarity when dealing with the questions of life. He has a gift for making the great truths very concise and practical. Rather than stirring himself each day to the tasks in hand, he basks in the goodness and love of his Lord. That, he says, is what gives him the strength he needs for what God has put on his plate that day. Let Jesus wash you. As he says, '*be blessed to be a blessing*'.

Don't feel embarrassed by this. He knows our weak human selves and it is His *pleasure* to wash your feet.

Just look at his talk with Peter (v8,9). Yes, it's true, having your feet washed is not all of it but it is our starting place.

Washing each other's feet (pooh!)

I have incredibly tickly feet. My wife only has to accidentally touch them in bed, and I jump through the roof. So, I really struggle with those moments in life where some well-meaning Christian has suggested, *'let's wash each other's feet'*. I know I'm going to go crazy and probably end up kicking the person in the face. I'm quite happy to be the one doing the washing, and not because I'm incredibly humble, I'm just too ticklish!

Yet Jesus is quite clear, it's what we're to do for each other (v13-15). Thankfully, and to help any unwanted moments of inexplicable violence, Jesus hits the root of it, *'Love one another. As I have loved you, so you must love one another. By this everyone will know that you are my disciples if you love one another'* (v34,35).

Three times it rings out, *'love one another'*.

I've seen that people who love God's family, warts and all, are truly reflecting Jesus. It's a way we know that he's in us. It must be, because frankly, we're usually the weirdest bunch of people around! John, in a later writing notes that anyone who says, *'I love God'*, but hates his brother is a *liar'* (1 Jn 4:20).

A mayor of a town further south than us was invited to visit a special church occasion. The family there were made up of around twenty different cultures and every age group there was. The mayor's jaw dropped as he sat through the morning. He said that he'd never come across a place in France where so many different peoples and ages lived together in peace.

Love the family of Jesus. Love the family **He** has chosen.

Have their backs. Watch out for them. Cry when they cry and laugh when they laugh. Be slow to criticise and quick to encourage. Judas didn't only betray Jesus; he betrayed the whole group.

And to wrap it up ...

What has all this got to do with listening? A lot.

Judas spent three years with Jesus. He saw and heard it all, yet he didn't listen. We can see all the amazing things God is doing around the world, in our own lives, in our church and yet, still not listen.

When Jesus is talking to you, through whatever means, make sure that you are not just hearing words but are listening so that you too, along with Peter, say '*you are the Christ, the Son of the living God'*.

Virginie hated the idea of moving. She was happy and content where she lived. Her children were trying to persuade her and her husband to move closer to the family and to an apartment. She'd never 'grown old' and had remained a young girl in her heart, so this idea of no longer being able to manage her home in a village seemed alien.

To put the matter to rest and stop the nagging of her children, she said if God would sell her house for the figure she wanted and the apartment could be bought for the offer she'd made (it was ridiculously low) within a few days, she'd believe it was God's will.

It happened within a day. Though not overly pleased with the response from God, Virginie has always had the confidence that this was his move, he had spoken.

The new home was in a centre of retirement apartments. An unexpected decline in her husband's health, and a life-giving group of other Christians she's found there has made this the right move at the right time.

One of the great joys in life ... is just being with people you love.

John Chapter 14
Hanging out with Jesus

We live at the edge of one of Europe's premier Nordic ski areas. From December through to early March you can see people of all ages enjoying the circuit which goes on up through our valley, La Clarée, past the adjoining villages to the end. It covers around 65km of which we proudly control around 12km. Our part is a great spot, with events, restaurant, shops, sledging area and a snowshoe walking track. Each day the snow is carefully groomed, temperatures are taken with all the appropriate signs filled in, the pass office is tidied and the guards stand ready to help emergencies. We have large numbers of visitors each year that enjoy our mix of mountains and cross-country skiing.

I learnt recently that an entire season of this activity, all that effort and investment only equate to one day's turnover in the main snow area of Montgenèvre. Suddenly it all seems very small and almost irrelevant.

This chapter does exactly that.

Jesus had told them in the previous chapter that he was leaving them, that he'd be betrayed by one of them. They must have been feeling very low. What was all this about? They'd left everything to follow him, now he was going to leave them. What would happen to them? What'd been the point of it all?

The Way, the truth, the life

Jesus opens with those amazing words, *'do not let your hearts be troubled. Believe in God, believe also in me'* (v1). Here is another moment when we see that believing in Jesus is so much more than just acknowledging his existence. It's believing in who *he* is, what *he* said, and where *he* is heading. He doesn't just say 'stop worrying,' but replace it with 'believing.'

This belief carries with it not just the things you need day by day but your eternal existence (v3). It is so much more than we understand. But it's why each one of his disciples, according to church tradition, happily gave their lives up for this person. They got it. They understood that like us in the Nordic skiing area in my village, that this life with all its worries and concerns was only like one day in the turnover of the main area. It was not worth comparing with what Jesus had in mind.

Have you been in those prayer meetings where all the requests are about jobs or health issues or financial problems? How rarely do we hear prayers that say, 'Lord I want to know you more,' 'Lord, I want my heart to be your home'. They sound irrelevant and impractical but are of far greater value than the former ones. I like to break prayers or life down into three areas (I know this has been covered in chapter 4 to a level but it's worth repeating):

- **Level 1**. The basics. These are the daily needs we have. Food, health, finance etc. If we ask people how they are we generally get an answer at this level. I often think of it as the great deflector of real issues. Business, tiredness and ill health are great

They are not 'how you are,' for that you need to go to another level.

- **Level 2**. The next step. How are you? 'Not so good, I'm terrified of admitting to my wife we've got no money.' Or 'I've fallen out with a colleague and can't seem to put it right'. These speak of an awareness of the more important issues in our lives. We become aware of the building blocks that are the foundation of our day to day. None of us operate well if our relationships are broken. Yet, there is another level that underpins them all.

- **Level 3**. This level relates to how we are living our core values. How are you? 'Struggling with feeding off God at present,' would be an answer at this level, or 'finding patience a hard virtue to come by'. Now we're getting somewhere. These are the areas that drive level 1 and 2 and put the right perspective on it. Learn to base your life in level 3 and you'll follow the well-known verse 6, *'I am the way, the truth and the life'*.

When Jesus and his life are at our core. When he is the engine that motivates and directs our homes, our relationships and our lives, our world will change.

Jesus, our home designer

Health issues have never been far from my wife and I, and although difficult to go through, they have taught us that this life isn't the end. We no longer have a bucket list that we 'must do' here, thinking it will be our only chance. 'Oh, we have to get to such and such a place before we die,' seems so irrelevant compared to the incredible excitement of what Jesus is saying here, 'I'm the one getting it ready for you,' (v2).

I'm always glad when a certain member of our staff is preparing an apartment for arriving guests. I know not only will it be done well, but that the incoming client will go, 'wow!' Those little touches, the way their towels are laid out, the chocolate carefully placed, the inviting looking bed after a long journey and so on. Isn't it incredibly exciting that Jesus himself is the one who is preparing our place? Is there any experience on this planet that could compare to Jesus getting your room ready (v2)?

'Have you been or done this or that?' It all seems very tame and flat next to 'I have a home Jesus is personally getting ready for me,' (v2). Like our little Nordic ski area, it is dwarfed by something so much greater.

But it gets better, and at this point you really can put down all the 'must do' experience guides you have.

I'm coming to get you

One of the great joys in life, and the French are so good at this, is just being with people you love. Usually, it is around a meal and here they can go on for hours.

When we arrived in France, we had a problem. The French-owned chalets we would rent for our clients. They rarely had comfortable seating areas. Instead, they would have the mother of all tables in pride of place with just a poky two-seater sofa in a corner. This didn't meet with the expectation of British clients who'd like to sit back comfortably and watch a film or something. When we tried to persuade the French owners that they needed to invest in comfortable seating they seemed puzzled. Surely a holiday was all about sitting round a table and talking, about 'being with each other'.

Jesus said that I'm coming to get you so that we can be together (v3). Although He is the eternal Son of God, he is also forever Jesus, with nail prints in his hands and feet. He wants to be with us. Maybe there will be no comfortable seating and films in his place. He does promise a feast (Rev 19:9) and if Jewish wedding traditions were anything to go by, they last a long time.

Every yearning in us, even the longing for experiences and thrills are found in this man. *'When you have seen me, you've seen my Father,'* he said to a puzzled Philip (v8-10). Think about it, you've seen the very face of God, something forbidden to Jews. By following that 'knowing of God' in Jesus (v7) we're delving into the most amazing experience pool there is. Feeling lonely at times? He wants you. Feeling hopeless about the future? He's preparing our new home. Feeling distressed by not knowing where to go? He is the way, the truth and the life (v6).

I could go on all day. Everything we need, past, present and future is all wrapped up in Jesus. He is not the icing on the cake, he is the cake. This doesn't mean you shouldn't skydive, just put it in its place!

Just in case you forget ...

My nine-year-old son once famously said, when in trouble for yet another misdemeanour, 'I try to be good, but I keep forgetting.' Trying to keep a stern face whilst processing such an amazing answer was not easy. It's so, so true – of all of us.

Jesus said that we'd do greater works than him because he was going to the Father (v12). We could ask anything in His name, and he'd do it (v14). Not only would he do it but that it was to his Father's glory that it happened. This was not simply us giving it our best shot and hoping for the best.

I love armchair football. Having been well below average on the pitch, where my school sports teacher said, that 'if they paid money for a footballer's kneeing ability, I stood a chance', I still feel I've the right to comment with friends on every match, footballer and manager there is. Of course, I don't really. I'll never score that goal in the last minute of a cup final I dreamed about as a youngster. Jesus here is saying, not only will you be playing, but you'll be scoring the goals I made you to do.

Here's how ...

- Love Jesus with all your heart, your mind, your strength and your soul. What do you love most in life? Privacy, thrills, a person, your job, films? Look at how much energy you'll put into that thing to make sure it happens. Jesus is saying do the same for me (v15, 23). If you do, the Father and I will pop round for a bite to eat! (v23; Rv3:20)

- Keep his commands (v15). We'll come onto this in the next chapter as Jesus goes into exactly what his commands are. Suffice to say, the answer has little to do with you as an individual but you as part of his family. The promise is to his church.

- The Holy Spirit. It is by him, that we are (as a group) taught and reminded of what Jesus said (v26). It is he who lets us know we're not abandoned by God or 'left as orphans' (v18). Let the Holy Spirit have full access into your life, especially those 'my time' moments. It's through Him and by His power that we'll see the fulfilment of these verses.

Finally, Peace.

I'll finish this chapter with a bizarre idea.

The last line is about the prince of this world coming to get him (v26) and yet Jesus talks about leaving his disciples with peace (v27). If it was me, I'd say I'm leaving you determination, power and demon-bashing authority in this dark moment. No, it was 'peace' he was leaving.

Jesus perfectly understood the role of Satan. The enemy was allowed to do his work, to stir up hatred, to ensure Jesus was put to death, merely as an opportunity to show that Jesus loved his father. Again and again, you find that despite all the efforts of the evil one, he is no more than someone who fulfils the very plans of God. We don't fear him. We stay in the peace that Jesus gives.

We have pushed, shoved, struggled through many areas in our life only to look back and see the patient, peaceful hand of God consistently working out his plans. Many of the seeming great disappointments were, in fact, moments where God was saving us from ourselves and achieving *his* plans for our lives.

Peace, means being still and resting — even in a raging storm (Mt 8:23-27). Choosing to focus on Jesus and his words rather than panicking at life's events.

Practice it. Take time to be quiet with him. Every Sunday I try, more and more successfully, not to ask Jesus anything on my morning walk but just to enjoy Him.

I suspect I achieve more at that time than I'll ever realise.

Julie's world had fallen apart. A seemingly successful phase at church with people finding Jesus every week had fallen into division, backbiting and disaster. She was crushed. Having a passion for people inside and outside the church family, everything dear to her was disappearing.

Worse, she'd become angry and resentful of those who were to blame. She hated herself as she sensed she was becoming part of the problem and didn't know how to get out of it.

One day pouring her heart out to God she cried, 'Oh, I'm just so complicated Lord!' God replied instantly, 'You're not too hard for me'.

Those words electrified her. Not only did they give her peace and a way forward in the situation but they've frequently come back through life to strengthen her just when she needed it.

Our life, as a follower of Jesus, is this, knowing him and making him known to the world he put you in.

John Chapter 15
Don't Try Harder, Get closer

It was a Saturday, my wife was out at work, and I was home. She wasn't due back til late and I thought I would show her my amazing culinary skills by having a meal ready when she returned. I planned one of those slow cooker meals so it'd be ready whenever she finished her day.

I carefully added all the ingredients for a spectacular fusion of flavours and texture. What could go wrong! I left it to cook away feeling happy and smug. Coming back some hours later to check on the progress, I saw the meal sitting in the machine, stone cold and uncooked. Yes, you guessed it, I'd forgotten to switch the cooker on. The late start told, and rather than a deliciously tender meal served out as she walked in the door, she got a flustered husband and a chewy, raw kind of thing that despite her kind words was less digestible than the mountain boulders strewn around our valley.

This is what Jesus is saying here. The words which at the same time are stark yet full of promise hold the key to so much of our lives. It's basically, 'make sure you're plugged in'. Verse 5 encapsulates it, '*If you remain in me and I in you, you will bear much fruit; apart from me you can do **nothing**'.

I'm not an expert in viticulture but the audience Jesus was speaking to understood the image well. I live on the border of two of Europe's finest wine producing countries and I've seen enough vines to get what he was speaking about. I've seen the piles of dead branches put aside for burning and I've seen the seemingly harshly pruned ones still attached. I've seen the fruit they carry. I've also seen that the vine plant itself is not particularly attractive. It is a knobbly, strange tree which doesn't look like it would be capable of gracing the highest browed tables in the world with fine wine. Yet it is.

Many of us will know this passage well. However, knowing about something is very different from living it, a truth I discovered in my first attempts at skiing. It seems an obvious thing to say to a follower of Jesus, attach yourself to him and it'll all work out, but as we'll see it's not the easy path you're going on. Jesus called it the 'narrow gate' (Mt 7:13), a strange tree, but one that provides the most amazing fruit.

So why are we here? The big Q

The chapter ends with a little sentence that in a sense gives us the guide for why Jesus is talking as he does. '*You also must testify*, (about me)' (v27). We're not here to get through life, having had a successful career, good health, plenty of money, family and friends and great experiences.

In the great prayer in chapter 17:26 Jesus defines what he came to do, 'I have made **you** known to them'. The cross, the resurrection and everything else were all designed for this purpose: to bring us to the Father, to know **him.** Our life, as a follower of Jesus, is this, knowing **him** and making **him** known to the world he put you in.

We'll never understand what happens when we're attached to the vine unless we understand this truth. Being in the vine will make you fruitful but you'll bear the grapes that come from the DNA of the vine. They'll be no pears or oranges coming, just the grapes that come from his DNA. However, they are the best and will go on to do more to change the world than anything else. What's more, we'll play the exact part that each of us was designed for.

The great blood transfusion ...

When people have a serious blood disorder, they often need a transfusion. The old blood is taken out and the new put in. We're looking for a Jesus transfusion in our lives by being plugged into him.

The alternative, Jesus said, is to wither and die (v2,6). Maybe we're someone who hangs around with followers of Jesus but don't ourselves believe that he is *our* Lord. If so, we will never bear fruit.

I remember being quizzed by a church leader when we arrived in France (a really nice guy) about exactly what we had and hadn't done (baptism etc). Once we'd correctly ticked all the boxes, we had quite a good time together but it's not the way to see if someone is walking with Jesus or not. Jesus is far more practical, 'Do they have my life in them and bear fruit or are they dead?' (v5,6).

Yummy fruit!

What is this fruit? Is it those who do great miracles? People who can prophesy or preach in a way that makes us tingle all over? I'd suggest from this passage and others, certainly not. The fruit we're to look for is love, joy, peace, forbearance, kindness, goodness, faithfulness, gentleness and self-control,' (Gal 5:22). Yes, great healings and signs will come too, but without the fruit they're no more than a deception (Rev 13:13-14), more on this later.

In chapter one, John declared that they had seen his glory, one who was full of '*grace and truth*' (1:14). If the signs we see do not have this behind us, they're of no value.

Don't get me wrong, we're not put on earth just to be 'nice' people. We're here to be people who challenge the very fabric of our societies and call people to follow the greatest revolutionary of all time.

One of the signs that you're doing it right is that you'll be hated just like Jesus (v18-19). I personally find this tough. Living as a foreigner in a country it's easy just to try to blend in whereas I've been called here to be part of the family that brings Jesus to a thirsty nation.

'Do as you are told!'

'Do as you're told!' words my dad used to bark out to me when I'd been caught doing something wrong yet again. When Jesus says, '*obey my commands*', he wonderfully ties it into 'remaining in my love'. Following his commands is about staying in his love (v10). I don't remember thinking, 'I must try to stay in my dad's love a little more,' when I got the justified telling off.

When I thought that 'obeying his commands' was about praying harder, giving more, getting up earlier, I felt ready to be thrown into the fire along with all the other dead branches. I would just never measure up to those great Christians who seemed so much better at those things. My lack of love for my alarm would surely spell my doom. How wrong was I.

Look again at the verses. See what happens when we get close, they're nothing like the alarm clock saga:

- v7 'ask for whatever you wish and it will be done for you.' His desires become our desires and our answers to prayer will multiply.

- v10. We'll remain in his love. Does that mean he stops loving us when we do it wrong? No, remaining in his love is like soaking in a hot bath. You're completely immersed in a man who '*loved me and gave his life for me*' (Gal 2:22). You're passionately loved in any and every situation of life, past and present and into a future where he has gone before and made a place for me. Remain in that love. Yes, you can start grinning now!

- v11. You'll experience a joy that has nothing to do with life's events. It is a complete joy that no-one can ever take away from you. This doesn't mean we don't cry at times or people won't hate us but rather that we're wrapped up in the one who for the '*joy set before him, endured the cross, despising its shame'* (Heb 12:2).

- v12-13,17. Here's the blockbuster that set me whooping for joy and liberated me from all religious effort, '*love one another as I have loved you'*. This was our goal. Not prayer meetings, missions, fasts and so on. It was simply to '*love each other as I have loved you'*. And guess what, the more time I'm plugged into Jesus the more I want to love. This one we'll look at later.

- v14-15. He calls us friends! Imagine it, the Lord of all creation, of eternity says to me, 'James, you're my friend'. And he cleaned up this unworthy life with his own blood so he could say those world-shattering words. Stay plugged in! It's great, isn't it?

- v16. You did not choose me but I chose you. This hits at the heart of everything religious. At school I was nearly always last when other classmates were given the job of choosing teams for a sporting event. I hated it. The only argument they had over me seemed to go:

  - Team 1 captain: 'You have him.'

  - Team 2 captain: 'No, you have him.'

  - I was evidently not sought after for my sporting prowess. We are **HIS** choice. It doesn't change if you're a failure in so many areas. We are his decision. Our only job is to stay plugged in.

Love, the greatest of all

The old tent maker called this the greatest of all attributes without which none of the others had any value (1 Co 13:1-3). When love drives us rather than any other motive it will define our actions and our choices in life. Our giving, our time, our prayer, our spreading the good news, our gathering together with his people – all these things will be different when motivated by love, rather than guilt or some religious sense of duty.

Yes, I know that there are days when we do things out of duty rather than love. It takes me some minutes to adjust when I turn off a movie at its climax to talk to someone calling who needs help. But I still don't do it because I ought to, I do it because this is the path of love and it's so much better than any path I've ever trod.

We looked previously at the importance of starting each day by knowing we are loved. Being blessed makes us a blessing, remember? The following empty lines are the time for you to go and do whatever it is you do to relax. However, this time I want you to do it plugged into Jesus. Into someone who was prepared to 'empty himself of everything but love,' as Charles Wesley put it, to get you. Not just to get you, but to let you know, he's always been after you, always wanted you. And he's done what's necessary to get you cleaned and ready to spend eternity in the most unimaginably delightful existence that there is.

(Have those other means of 'relaxation' lost a bit of their shine?)

When you do this, you'll pray more, sing more, give more, be more.

That's what love does.

And so ...

This being plugged in is all about letting his life flow through you, individually and as a group. Here are four simple ways (yes, I know, you'll have heard it all before in other chapters!).

1. Give *time* to him. Make space in your day away from distractions, so you can understand what being plugged in means for you and those around you. It'll become your special 'us' time. You'll resent it being interrupted.

2. Consciously make him a part of all that you do. Preparing a talk, preparing a meal; Brushing up on your Bible or brushing your teeth; sitting with a lonely pensioner or sitting in front of the telly. You'll find that things you don't want him to be there for become more obvious and uglier.

3. Read his great book (the Bible). See his teachings and see his life. Look at what happened in the early church. See the story of the greats like Noah, Abraham, Jacob, Moses, Ruth, David, Esther and so on. See how weak we were in ever following God by rules. There are many good reading plans out there but maybe start by asking the Holy Spirit to show you what to read.

4. Be actively a part of his people. You'll never hear him properly without being in a functioning body. This is where the Holy Spirit will be very active (v26) (here called the Advocate – yes, someone's pleading our cause before the highest court in the universe!).

All of these are doorways that enable listening. We'll be plugged into his plans and purposes for your area. I know he has great plans for the people of my country.

Hearing what he's saying to us, through us and around us will mean we'll bear fruit that will make the finest wine there is.

Julian had always wanted to work with wood. He was never happier than when he was making an item from this amazing material. He lived in an apartment and had a family so in reality it was nothing more than a pipe dream, but it was one he gave to God with a cry from his heart.

The years passed and jobs came and went. He took special courses to train in furniture making but nothing ever opened up. The other jobs never seemed to work out either.

One day God spoke to him from Exodus 3:17 that it was time to leave and go to another place 'a place flowing with milk and honey'. The journey was still a long one but after another move he came to a village where he was given a workshop and friends who helped bring his vision to life.

He now runs a furniture making business that he loves and has brought delight to many homes around.

There is always room for so much more. Don't stop asking.

John Chapter 16
The Player Manager

Sometimes in a sporting club you get an individual who'll have two jobs. They're called the player/manager. Not only do they direct, coach and build the team, they lead them on the pitch as well. They get to select the team and they get to play in it (assuming they've selected themselves!). Footballing legends like Gianluca Vialli of Chelsea is a great example.. Here the Holy Spirit is portrayed like this.

The Holy Spirit is not in heaven waiting but has been specifically sent to help the church play the role the Father has called it to (v7,8,13). Do you feel like you or your team don't quite match up to what God has called us to be? I know I have and I still do.

Enter the Holy Spirit.

He was sent not only to continue the upheaval in society that Jesus made, but to take it worldwide. His job of convicting the world we live in of '*sin, righteousness and judgement*,' (v8), involves taking on the vested powers of unbelief, self-worth that is Christless, and the Devil himself. He does not do this in a vacuum or away from the family of God, but he is very much on the pitch with us, playing the game. He's reminding us of what team we're playing for, our abilities in God, of the limitless possibilities when we believe, and who our real enemy is.

If you don't have a strong connection with the Holy Spirit, you'll play a very weak game. Imagine the ludicrous

149

situation of a player ignoring the lead and cries of his captain and manager. That player will soon be substituted. It is vital that the rest of the team listen to and follow him.

I remember a school sporting day when my four-year-old son was taking part in the pre-schoolers race. The starting cry went up and the little guys charged down the track. Well, not all. One of them, head down, and eager to win the race by means of staring at their feet, shot off in completely the wrong direction. If he'd been on the right track, I think he might have won it. I remember he covered a huge distance at great speed, taking no notice of my yells.

If we don't allow the Holy Spirit to lead us as a church, as families or as individuals, we'll never run the race that God has set for us (2 Tim 4:7).

How does he coach me?

This connection with the Holy Spirit is vital. Let's have a look at what he does in this chapter:

- He is the 'advocate'. Pleading not just for us but also for the cause of Jesus Christ and his radical kingdom (v7). Whoop!

- He will 'prove the world wrong about sin' (v8). I'm suspicious of any 'truth' that Christians buy into that has not originated within Jesus' family or is clear in scripture. There's a pattern whereby, in response to the norms of our society, the church feels it needs to accommodate them and even build it into a theology. We 'Christianise' the opinions of non-believers and claim them to be ours. Be wary of the roots and origins of any 'truth' that you hear and any ideology that places your feelings above God's. It's sure to go wrong. We plug into *him* and not him into *us* (previous chapter and Rm 1:25).

- He will prove the world wrong about 'righteousness' (v8). One of my most liberating experiences in life was realising that I had no merit of my own. I'd nothing to bring to the table that would do me any good before God. I was a broken and ruined version of what God had created. This has meant that the death and resurrection of Jesus are everything to me. The new life and identity I now have is beyond argument because none of it relies on me. It relies totally on his words, his actions, his promises. It's a huge relief when we get it. We really can't lose! Self-righteousness or 'being happy with who you are', is one of the big deceptions of our society. I've made the mistake of trying to soften the blow to people who are seeking God about just how sinful sin is. It's ended in tears. If people don't know where their goodness and self-worth is based, they'll never be strong in faith.

- He will prove the world wrong about 'judgement' (v8). This is particularly focused on the '*prince of this world*' (v11), a name given to the devil. All the enemy's works to 'rob, kill and destroy' (10:10), are undone by the work of the Holy Spirit. When healing comes into broken homes, food into famine, hope into despair. It's the Holy Spirit working through his people to bring 'judgement' on Satan's reign of terror.

- He will guide us into all the truth (v13). The Holy Spirit not only oversaw the writing of the Bible, but he also makes it alive and powerful to the people of God. He gives us an understanding of what is right and wrong. One of the gifts of the Holy Spirit given to the church in 1 Cor 12 is the discerning of Spirits. My wife uses it. So often fine sounding arguments get unmasked quickly as nothing more than ramblings or demonically inspired thoughts by this gift. Trust Him not only in the scriptures that he will bring them to life but that he will also bring truth to your current situation and circumstances. It's his job.

- He will glorify Jesus (v14). Here is a great test to see if something has come from the Holy Spirit or not. Does it make Jesus look great? This is his job. Like Jesus on earth, he does nothing that he's not been told to do (v13-15). Have you heard people say, 'the Spirit told me such and such'? Well, here is one of the tests to see if it is true. Does what's been said or done bring glory to Jesus or not? Despite people's best efforts to make this complicated, it really isn't.

- He will tell you what is yet to come (v13). The gift of prophecy, interpreting events and foretelling the future can seem very mystical. Many of us have heard prophecies that have predicted the end of time, the second coming, the world collapse and so on. During the Covid pandemic they reached fever proportions (no pun intended). How do we know what's true? Remember what the aim of the Holy Spirit is. He's not an author of fear or one who gets us to run away from life. Just the opposite, he calls us into a battle that may cost our lives (v2,33). Like Jesus, we'll be thrust into the limelight as we declare a Kingdom that blows away fear and hatred. If the prophecies you're hearing do not do the above, they are not from the Holy Spirit. Ignore them.

How do I link with the Holy Spirit?

The Holy Spirit is the birth right of every child of God. It is not for the spiritual or the mature. Acts 2 & 7 shows that he was given as people first believed. Acts 10 at Cornelius' house shows it was given before people had done the correct 'believing and repenting courses!'. People who received Him, took on some extraordinary, supernatural things. Jesus said to his disciples to 'wait' until they had received the promised gift from the father (Acts 1:4). I know that there are many discussions on how this relates to us today. But let me just say this, if you feel a lack in your life of his supernatural presence, ask. The early church apostle Paul encouraged his readers to '*be being filled with the Spirit*' (Eph 5:18). It was a continuous process. Whatever your understanding is, there is always room for so much more.

Don't stop asking. Ask God directly. Ask others you trust.

And to finish ...

The chapter finishes with a great double statement, '*in this world you will have trouble. But take heart! I have overcome the world*' (v33).

Thanks for the heads up, Jesus, I'll try not to be surprised at problems (even if I don't like them).

Problems and difficulties are a guarantee. So is the complete victory in life that we have in him.

Jon didn't want to be part of the dating game. Life was too short. As a 16-year-old he'd prayed long and hard that God would show him what to do early in life. He didn't want to waste time chasing.

Emily walked into the place he was working one day. His jaw dropped. She was the one.

Frightened he might be making a mistake he prayed long and hard, asking God for a clear sign. He didn't normally do this, but it was too important to leave to chance.

His route to work took him along a path into town and he asked God that if she was the right one, she'd be the first person he'd meet. There were often people on this route, so it was a big ask.

That day, no-one was on the journey until he'd nearly arrived at work. Around a corner Emily suddenly appeared and stood in front of him. She was meant to be elsewhere that morning, but circumstances had changed her programme. God had spoken.

This was the woman for him. Twenty years on and three children later, she still is.

The devil's priority is to divide us.

John Chapter 17

The Keys to Life

I quite enjoy listening to people in the 'three wishes' game. You know the one where you think of the three best things you could ask for. I remember as a child wishing for 'all the sweets in the sweet shop'. As I grew up it moved to scoring the winning goal at a cup final and onto the Ferrari Dino 246GT. As the years go by, the wishes change.

What are your three wishes? Here Jesus gives his (well, it's actually four but he's allowed as many as he wants). They are very different to the human ones but given that he knows what life is really about, we do well to take them to heart and set our course in the same direction.

Prayer One: To actively and vividly know you (v1-5)

His first one was that He might be glorified. This is a strange request from our viewpoint. Whether we think a lot of ourselves or not, none of us would ever dare say this. We hear the politician basking in his success, saying 'Oh no, it was the team around me!' even if he doesn't mean it. Yet here is Jesus, asking to be glorified (v1) with the same glory he had before when he was with the Father (v5). Here Jesus gives the clue as to why he's asking to be glorified, it's '*so that your Son may glorify you,*' (v1). This was his life's passion.

Jesus doesn't need everyone to know how great he was because he had an ego problem.   No, to be glorified meant something so much more.

I remember my father training me to plant baby cabbages. He'd say, 'Now watch carefully Jimmy, see how I space and plant them. I want you to do the same'. (I remember asking him to repeat the demonstration several times so that there would be fewer cabbages for me to plant.) He wanted me to mirror his actions.

To glorify something is to give as exact a representation as possible. So, to 'glorify' a great painting in this context would be to represent it accurately and fully describe its beauty and composition. Here, Jesus was asking for that to be the exact representation of his Father. He'd had this before the world was created (v5). He and the father were an exact reflection. The ultimate perfection and beauty expressed in the trinity.

He was about to go through the '*hour that has come,*' (v1), to lay down His life so that we could have real and eternal life. He wanted to be the mirror image of God to the world. (Cl 1:15; Hb 1:3). The glory of an eternal self-existent, complete God, freely laying down his life for people like us. Wow!

Life, but not as we know it …

Eternal life. 'To live forever' funnily enough often appears in people's wishes as they grow older. We sometimes see dictators grimly clinging onto power well into their old age, they wish it would go on forever. Here Jesus gives eternal life as a free gift to those '*his Father had given him,*' (v6).

What is the eternal life Jesus was talking about? Is it more of what we have here just longer. Not a bit. Jesus explains it as 'to **know you**, the only true God, and Jesus Christ, whom you have sent,' (v3).

To *know* something today doesn't mean much. 'I already know that,' the cocky child says, meaning, 'I don't need to be told anything, I'm already clever'. This isn't that. To 'know' here (the Greek word is a verb *ginosko*) is an active, vivid word that you might use in the following context:

'I've broken my ribs and it really hurts when I cough.'

'I *know* what you mean, it *happened* to me last year.'

There is an active and vivid attachment to the knowledge of that experience because you'd felt the pain too.

Jesus is saying that our 'active and vivid' attachment to his Father **is** eternal life. The one who has no beginning or end, the one who is the source of all that is good in life, the one who loved you and sent his only son to take you into his family. *Knowing him,* that is all you'll ever want. It's the ultimate buzz we'll ever have, and it will eternally get better and better (10:10).

I live in some of the most majestic scenery in Europe with some of the most exhilarating experiences available. It's all a candle on a bright summer's day compared to knowing God.

Don't miss it. It was a great joy to Jesus (v6-8) that his disciples understood and experienced it. He wants that for us as well.

Prayer Two: That they are protected v11,12,15

This is a funny prayer, after all who'd dare pick a fight with God? Plenty do, and in case you get all indignant about it, we did as well. We're described as his 'enemies' before he took us on board (Rom 5:10; Col 1:21). One of the great proofs to me of the truth of Jesus is the irrational hatred he inspires in so many. Somebody, something, somewhere hates him.

The current wave of films that display the pagan as the 'cool' guy (haircut and all), and the Christian as the warped, manipulative evil person is a lie of real history, but it says something about the human heart. *'We'll not have this man reign over us,'* (Lk 19;14) is still a current song.

I've often forgotten to pray this prayer of protection, even though it's in the words Jesus taught, *'deliver us from the evil one,'* (Mt6:13). I know that we're told to *'be alert and of sober mind. Your enemy the devil prowls around like a roaring lion looking for someone to devour,'* (1 Pt 5:8). If Jesus thinks we should do it, it's a good idea.

The reason is given in verse 11, and what we're really praying about when asking for protection, and this leads us onto wish 3.

Prayer Three: A united people with one heart v21

Verse 11 says, '*Holy Father, protect them by the power of your name, the name you gave me, so that they may be one as we are one*'. The intimate unity of Father and Son was integral to the life of Jesus on earth. It's integral to us, his family. Importantly, it forms a huge part of our listening to God. We need each other more than we know, and we'll never get unity with God without unity with each other. The two are integrally bound up (v21).

One of the greatest evidences of the devil's work is not Christians being beaten up and left for dead (that's actually a cause of rejoicing but that's another book!), it is the disunity amongst his people.

The Father and the Son are one, perfect in unity. It's impossible to try and split where the Father starts, and the Son stops. Many people have had a go, but we inevitably trip up as the Father and the Son are just too close, they are one. This is as it should be and is what he wants for us, his people (v21).

When we realise it is the devil's primary work, to divide and scatter the sheep of Jesus, we're on our guard.

In the local town, where I live, there is a long history of a divided church, of Christians scattered all over, criticising and tearing at each other. Wonderfully it is beginning to change but it's taking time. I know, it's true, we're probably the most weird and strange group of people you could find. Yet v23 stands*, 'I in them and you in me – so that they may be brought to complete unity. Then the world will know that you sent me and have loved them even as you have loved me'*.

Unity is not just a mushy, kum-by-yah feeling, but an essential part of the world seeing and 'actively and vividly' knowing that Jesus is who *he* said *he* is.

Now do you see why the devil's priority is to divide us? It kills the clarity of our message. The message is what he hates the most and a divided church is the best way to mute it.

Prayer Four: Get dressed, we're going out (v17-19)

'Sanctify' is one of my least favourite words. It reminds me of my mother 'sanctifying' my ears as a child by removing days of built-up grime with a firm hand, soap and a scratchy towel (she had six children so every few days was the best she could do). However, she never did it because I wanted to go and play in the garden, she did it because we were going out somewhere important. Maybe to visit someone, or to church, who knows? I only remember the discomfort. She, however, was preparing me for the journey we were about to undertake.

We don't need cleaning up because Jesus' work on the cross was not enough or somehow lacking, (we'll look at that in the next two chapters). I really don't need to be made any more 'righteous,' Jesus has done it all (v2). Yet, we still need to be sanctified. Even Jesus said he'd done it (v19), so it really can't be to make you more righteous. Don't let religious types beat you up on this.

The reason Jesus said, 'I sanctify myself' (v19) was because he had a job to do and the chosen discipline of the journey to the cross (wholly unnecessary except for love) 'sanctified' him.

Jesus said in v18 'I have sent *them* (that's you and me) into the world.' So, we also have a job to do, it's to pass on the message, telling people about Jesus (not the other list of things Christians can get hung up on). It's the only way you and I ever came to know Christ. Someone, somewhere told us. To be set apart for this job means we must be 'sanctified by his truth.' In other words, we preach the 'good news of Jesus Christ,' and not necessarily one that includes the socially acceptable sound bites. We're set apart to be *his messengers* in whatever field he's placed us.

I saw a powerful Easter message broadcast from the Houses of Parliament in the UK. The message was simply Bible readings about the Easter story. What made it unusually powerful was that it was given by people from all sides of politics who'd united around one person, Jesus Christ, and what he's done.

Sanctification helps us make him look good. A life as a drunk, a gossiper, sexually immoral, a divisive person etc distorts the message. We're not told to stop hanging round those people because they don't agree with us (1 Co5:11) but because their sin is *clouding* Jesus from other people's eyes. Our job is to make him shine, wherever we are, whatever we're doing. Yes, it might make people react badly (as did the demons to Jesus) but others will start to follow.

Let him change you by his truth so that *he'll* shine out of your life. Get sanctified: drink up your bible, talk to Jesus, sing to and enjoy him, hang out with people who have the same passion.

And to finish …

Guys, this is it. This is what Jesus wanted to be glorified for. Here is ultimate experience, ultimate beauty, ultimate joy and wonder. Why else do we do things in life, if not searching for these things? He's made the way that we are fully part of everything he has, co-heirs (v24).

Let his four prayers become yours as well.

Jean-Michel was fed up with arguing with his wife. A recent stroke had left him volatile, and he quickly lost his temper. He knew it was wrong and asked God to help.

He didn't get one great answer but what he did learn was to ask God what to do every time he seemed to be losing control. It wasn't an immediate process but grew little by little. God gave him many answers and showed him how he could love his wife and bring peace into the home. Strokes were not too complicated for God.

Rather than drift apart as many stroke patients have talked about, his marriage today is beautiful and strong. He still has his moments, but he knows where to go for help.

If you are going to be of any use to God, don't be too surprised when it all goes badly wrong.

John Chapter 18
When it all goes wrong

The next chapters roll into each other so I'm going to focus in this chapter on the situation Peter found himself in. As we'll see, listening to Jesus doesn't necessarily mean we take any notice of what he says. This is particularly true if it's something we don't want to hear.

Peter had become a leader amongst the disciples of Jesus. He was one of the three close ones taken to some special places and moments; he had the profound revelation that Jesus really was the Messiah, and that this messiah was the Son of God (Mt 16:16). That he was the older brother and in charge of the family fishing business seems obvious from the text. He comes across as a man who'd take charge. The fact he still had a sword by his side after spending three years on the road with Jesus speaks of someone who, whilst he believed, felt his job was still to protect him. At one moment at the end Jesus had told them to take a sword (Lk 22:35-38) it's funny that they already had two. I'm sure Peter had one of them.

What did he make of Jesus predicting his denials? (13:36-38). Probably as much as I did when someone said to me as a twelve-year-old boy, 'James, don't take that bike apart, you'll never get it back together'. I didn't believe them. I could do it just fine. It turns out that they were right, and the bike remained in its 162 constituent parts until it was unceremoniously dumped.

I could recount many other such words as I'm sure you could. Peter was a classic bravado man, *'even if all fall away, I never will,'* (Mt26:33). I'm sure the other disciples felt he had their backs.

Why did he have to go through this?

Jesus highlighted something in Peter's character that would inevitably want to protect him, *'I'll lay my life down for you,'* was how he genuinely felt. But this very act of passionate loyalty to Jesus would stop him from being of any use.

Did you really hear that? I'll say it again, the very act of passionate loyalty to Jesus that Peter had would stop him of being any real use to God. Wow! I thought we had to be like that to be good at our mission!

It wasn't that Peter didn't really mean it, after all he cut off the servant's ear (v10) trying to defend Jesus. (He was either displaying a master stroke of swordsmanship, or more likely from a fisherman, it was just a bad swipe. Thankfully, Jesus sorted the situation out, as he does. See LK 22:51.)

Although Jesus had been confronted and threatened many times before, this is the first time he'd been physically bound and led away. The soldiers, priests and Pharisees hadn't gained the upper hand, it was simply that Jesus said, *'shall I not drink the cup my Father has given me,'* (v11). It was *now* his time. Peter still didn't get what was happening, he'd promised he'd go with Jesus to death. For him everything was going wrong!

I expect he was deeply confused by what was happening. Should he follow and still try to lay his life down for his

Messiah? Or just see if Jesus would walk away free as he'd done before?

Whatever his thoughts were, God's preparation of Peter to lead the first charge of the church was taking place.

The Denials

The denial wasn't just a little one by all accounts. It wasn't a mumbled apology of 'I don't know what you're talking about'. It was accompanied by declaring he'd never known Jesus, swearing, as only a fisherman knew how, with oaths and curses that would probably make us shiver.

It wasn't even as if Jesus wasn't in trouble. His Lord, his friend (v15), his personal messiah who'd been waited for, for centuries, was going to be put to death and all Peter could do was blindly swear that he meant nothing to him.

He'd been up all night, exhausted and cold, (Mt 26:43; v18). The cock crowed. Now he was broken.

This was a big time mess up. If he was in today's church leadership, he would undoubtedly be put into the quiet place where failed church leaders go and are never heard of again. Here Jesus is getting him ready to lead off his new kingdom message.

But why did it take this?

When I was 30, myself, my wife and family left for a life in India. A pattern of prophecies and circumstances, together with counsel from the wisest, had shown us that this was the right course. We sold everything up in the UK and left '*to fulfil the purposes of God*'.

We stayed there just over a year. What a nightmare.

From our work with the church, to our business, and finally my wife's health, everything that could fall apart did. We came back to Britain after a year, broken people. The doctors advised against my wife travelling for at least six months because of her poor health. We'd started a business in India to support our work and now we were stranded, penniless, confused and distraught. We had three young children, no home and no job. I found myself crying out 'why God?'.

The Holy Spirit whispered to me, 'James, now you're ready'. We went on to work in a church as a pastor, my wife as an evangelist. It turned out to be the most fruitful phase we'd ever experienced.

God must break us sometimes from our own abilities before we can do the work that he's planned for us. He has to teach us to be listeners and work with him and not from our own resources. A verse became very relevant to us both:

His pleasure is not in the strength of the horse,

nor his delight in the legs of the warrior;

the LORD delights in those who fear him,

who put their hope in his unfailing love.

(Psalm 147:10-11)

We'll look at Peter's restoration in chapter 21, but I love the fact that the book of John not only covers the prediction, the actual denials but also how Jesus puts him back together.

If you are going to be of any use to God, don't be too surprised when it all goes badly wrong, including when you mess up big time.

God doesn't need your abilities, he wants you.

Finally ...

There is not the slightest inkling here that Jesus is out of control in any of the events. He heals up the ear cut off (Mk 14:47), he makes sure all his followers are safe (v9) and he answers his accusers as much or as little as *he* wants. He's drinking his *Father's* cup not anyone else's (v11).

Your life is never out of control as a follower of Jesus. Even when everything around you is falling apart, there is not even a ripple in the sovereign purpose of Jesus to make sure you get to where you need to be, doing what he's made you to do. Stay in peace and keep your eyes on him.

Things going wrong don't mean you haven't been listening. Just the opposite. It may just mean you haven't understood. Even if you're going through the 'cross' moment and he's gone quiet, Jesus is still fully in control and knows exactly what he's doing.

Peter didn't listen to the warning. Maybe he was unable to until he'd gone through that terrible night.

Our dark nights are often his fastest roads.

Bernard was at a pastors' conference. A man prophesied over him that he would never build a large church but would be used to build thousands of small ones. At the time the 'how to grow your church' question was very big, so it was not the easiest thing to hear.

Since then, however, the work God has given him to do of distilling the basics of our faith into bite size pieces has enabled countless people to go on and establish teams, churches, businesses and projects in every area of life you'd care to think of. From governments down to a small house church. foundations are being built on the principles that last for eternity.

It's as he'd want it, he's still largely an unknown name. He just listened and obeyed. He still does.

Religion creeps in whenever we replace the immediacy of our relationship with Jesus by a set of rules.

John Chapter 18b and 19a
Slapping God in the Face

The next two chapters will deal with the trial, the crucifixion and burial of Jesus. Volumes have been written on this huge and central subject of our faith and to cover it in a few pages feels flippant and unworthy of the magnitude of the events. However, I'm going to draw out a few points which I trust will be valuable for us as followers of Jesus. There are many excellent books which cover the days in greater detail, and we'll have eternity to get our heads around this amazing moment of history.

The different groups of people act true to their nature. Jesus to the truth and above all to the will of his Father. The Jews' leaders to a bizarre mistaken religiosity that, as Jesus put it so well, made them '*strain a gnat but swallow a camel*' (Mt23:24). Finally, to Pilate and the Romans who represent the rest of the power/fear/rational tradition of the rest of the world.

Both the religious leaders and the Romans *slap* Jesus in the face (18v22; 19v2).

Slapping in the face in the Jewish culture was an insult. For a Roman to slap a Jew would also be designed to humiliate. It was usually done by a superior to an inferior (master/slave etc). At this time to do it to an equal was to break the law and incur a fine.

Here those who represent all aspects of humanity, which includes you and me, slap God in the face, saying to him 'We despise and insult you; you'll never reign over us'. We mock who he is and laugh, thinking at last he's under our control.

How wrong we were.

The religious leaders

Right from the arrest to the first trial (18:19-24;28) the religious leaders pretend to honour God, to have an open trial, to do the right thing. The reality was that the arrest was in secret and their trial happened in a closed place in the middle of the night. The truth is, they were scared. Jesus had trampled right through their religious world. The madness hits a crescendo in v28 where in order to be able to celebrate the Passover they wouldn't go into the Roman's place.

The very symbol of their Passover deliverance was a lamb slain with its blood put on their doorposts. Now here they were handing over God's real Passover lamb, their promised messiah to death. (Read Ex12:1-14 for the history, it's a great read.)

Religion in all its forms is opposed to God's real work. It's a cheap, nasty attempt at a copy but it completely distorts who God is and what he does. Remember it's at home in any kind of church: modern, traditional, small or large. It misses the point completely and worse, tries to kill off Jesus.

Religion creeps in wherever and whenever we replace the immediacy of our relationship with Jesus by a set of rules. How we should dress, our tone of voice when we pray, how we spend our time and so on. I remember when our church first got into dancing in the 1980s. We developed something called the 'charismatic hop'. It was a strange kind of dance, but it suited us British who'd never done that kind of thing. A new convert came to a meeting and was delighted to see we were allowed to dance in church; he started to groove out as he would at his nightclub. The slowly forming religious spirits in the meeting were sent flying! It was great.

They are like weeds in a garden, keep getting rid of them. They'll choke out the real voice of Jesus.

The Roman leaders

The leaders who represent the rest of non-religious people are different. They have that usual mix of irritation with religious problems (18v31), an attempt to be reasonable (18v38; 19v6), followed by compromise solutions (18v39), finally succumbing to fear of man that is greater than a fear of God (19v5-16).

The last three are so typical of the way the world tries to sort its problems. You can pick any event and they're usually there. I know I've done them many times, and I bet you have as well.

In the end, although we know what is right, we're too frightened by the consequences to follow it through. We end up in this horrible world of compromise where we end up slapping the face of God, so no-one slaps ours.

Those who don't do this are rare. However, there is hope. There was a third force at work in this trial; the one that was actually running the events.

God always gets the last say

There is no moment throughout the trial of Jesus where he was not fully aware that he was simply, if painfully, doing the will of his Father. His openness about his teaching in contrast to their deeds in the dark (18v21-22) showed this was no secret plan done in hiding. God's truth was out there in the open for all to hear. His commitment to the truth and his kingdom (18v23; 36) was just as his Father had shown him (5:19). This was not just some fanciful new idea but all these events down to small details had been predicted centuries before (19v11; 24;28;36-37). He was on *his* Father's agenda.

You might say, then the rest isn't our fault.

Wrong.

This doesn't exonerate our sin, Jesus makes this quite clear (v11), but it does mean that our sin cannot alter God's purpose. (Rom 9:19-26 is helpful on this.)

It is crucial for us to understand that God is in ultimate charge. It's why listening and walking with God is so fundamental. If Jesus had argued well, or stirred up the crowd on his side, or called down twelve legions of angels to rescue him (Mt 26:53), you and I would not be able to know the restoration of our relationship with God freely paid for at the crucifixion.

This is not to say Jesus was fatalistic and just rolled over. He knew he'd been sent for this very purpose (18v37). Many other times Jesus evaded arrest. He knew what was happening because he knew what he had to do. You and I were already engraved on his hands (Is 49:16).

It was obedience to his father and love for us that were to hold him on a cross, not the nails.

And to finish ...

Refuse to take on religious patterns that replace intimacy with Jesus. Even modern things that look different from how our fathers and grandfathers might have worshipped are just as religious if Jesus is not given his place at the head. In contrast some of the most traditional liturgies come to life when in the hand of the Holy Spirit.

Refuse the world's way of being reasonable, finding compromises and falling into fear at the expense of our wonderful Jesus. He was hated for who he was and so will we be. Get used to it and, like the apostles in Acts, even count it an honour, (Ac 5v41).

Finally, be deeply, deeply assured that our Father is the one fully in charge of our future. People can never determine our path in life, that's our Father's job alone.

JAMES HODSON

A couple had moved abroad to share Jesus. After a year they were asking God what they could do to be more effective in the place they were in as doors seemed to be tightly shut.

A woman who ran an agency in the town one day said, 'You have friends and I have properties. Let's work together.' They strangely but instantly knew it was God speaking.

They opened a company that grew and has enabled them to reach every part of the town they were in. Through that company they have seen people find Jesus, get baptised, and grow in their faith. They have seen it to be a blessing in the life of the town and its businesses.

God spoke through someone who didn't even know him.

*The plan of God was at work.
It always is.*

John Chapter 19b
The Miracle of the Murder

This section will be quite short for this book. I'm still left speechless by the events. The sheer physical agony of what Jesus faced dwarfed by the far greater spiritual pain of bearing my sin and facing the anger of his Father. The confidence that it was all still going according to the plan of him who calls all things into being. The truth that in my natural state I would have been baying for his blood along with many others. The little touches of making sure his mum was looked after. And finally, to the great earth-shattering statement '*it is finished*'. They're all so powerful. Too powerful.

That he chose the moment of his passing, confirmed by the soldier who came to break his legs but found him already dead (v33-34), was just proof that this was all part of the plan to get you and me to live with him.

I'm going to leave you to read the text again but invite you to take time to listen to the Holy Spirit as you do, and let him apply it to your life, to your group.

Then Pilate took Jesus and had him flogged. The soldiers twisted together a crown of thorns and put it on his head. They clothed him in a purple robe and went up to him again and again, saying, "Hail, king of the Jews!" And they slapped him in the face (19 v2,3).

Carrying his own cross, he went out to the place of the Skull (which in Aramaic is called Golgotha, (v17). There they crucified him, and with him two others – one on each side and Jesus in the middle (v18).

Pilate had a notice prepared and fastened to the cross. It read: JESUS OF NAZARETH, THE KING OF THE JEWS (v19). Many of the Jews read this sign, for the place where Jesus was crucified was near the city, and the sign was written in Aramaic, Latin and Greek (v20). The chief priests of the Jews protested to Pilate, 'Do not write 'The King of the Jews,' but that this man claimed to be king of the Jews' (v21).

Pilate answered, 'What I have written, I have written' (v22).

When the soldiers crucified Jesus, they took his clothes, dividing them into four shares, one for each of them, with the undergarment remaining. This garment was seamless, woven in one piece from top to bottom (v23).

'Let's not tear it,' they said to one another. 'Let's decide by lot who will get it' (v24).

This happened that the scripture might be fulfilled that said,

*'They divided my clothes among them
   and cast lots for my garment.''*

So this is what the soldiers did.

Near the cross of Jesus stood his mother, his mother's sister, Mary the wife of Clopas, and Mary Magdalene (v25). When Jesus saw his mother there, and the disciple whom he loved standing nearby, he said to her, 'Woman, here is your son, (v26) and to the disciple, 'Here is your mother,' (v27). From that time on, this disciple took her into his home.

Later, knowing that everything had now been finished, and so that Scripture would be fulfilled, Jesus said, 'I am thirsty' (v28). A jar of wine vinegar was there, so they soaked a sponge in it, put the sponge on a stalk of the hyssop plant, and lifted it to Jesus' lips (v29). When he had received the drink, Jesus said, 'It is finished'. With that, he bowed his head and gave up his spirit (v30).

Now it was the day of Preparation, and the next day was to be a special Sabbath. Because the Jewish leaders did not want the bodies left on the crosses during the Sabbath, they asked Pilate to have the legs broken and the bodies taken down (v31). The soldiers therefore came and broke the legs of the first man who had been crucified with Jesus, and then those of the other (v32). But when they came to Jesus and found that he was already dead, they did not break his legs (v33). Instead, one of the soldiers pierced Jesus' side with a spear, bringing a sudden flow of blood and water (v34). The man who saw it has given testimony, and his testimony is true. He knows that he tells the truth, and he testifies so that you also may believe (v35). These things happened so that the scripture would be fulfilled: 'Not one of his bones will be broken', (v36) and, as another scripture says, 'They will look on the one they have pierced' (v37).

The burial

Two religious leaders who'd let fear dominate their desire to openly follow Jesus came out of the woodwork to claim the body (v38-40). No longer frightened to be associated with Jesus, they made sure he was buried correctly before the fast-approaching Sabbath started. The amount of myrrh and aloes brought along is about double the amount normally given to notable people and four times the amount that was usual. In today's currency it would be over £125,000. This was a very profound moment in their life. Fear gave way to devotion.

The depths of despair felt by people who thought they were following the Messiah, God's own Son, must have been devastating. Everything had gone wrong. Everything was broken. Everything Jesus had stood against had won. I don't think we can ever imagine the desperate place his followers were in. There were no longer his words to comfort and guide them, to explain what was happening. Just horrible empty, brain-numbing silence.

They had no idea what was coming.

And to finish …

I will just encourage you that this moment of utter darkness for the disciples was also part of God's plan. They'd done nothing wrong. They couldn't have prayed more, believed more, given more. Nothing would have changed the course of this moment. It was simply the timing of God. Do not lose heart when all is broken around us. God is a God of resurrections.

The darkness of the death and burial of Jesus was to give way to something so glorious. The plan of God was at work. It always is.

Jenny and her husband have been through periods of tragedy, isolation, and darkness as part of their work in church leadership. When these have come via people she loved and trusted, and through lies and gossip, Jenny felt bereft, abandoned, and betrayed. The overwhelming disappointment and loneliness were a bitter dish to be served.

Since she'd been a child, she'd known God's faithfulness and knew that asking the 'Why?' and 'How?' questions served little purpose. She also knew that as a daughter of God, she was not a victim, because God hadn't stopped loving her or working in the situation. However, she also knew that the enemy was out to steal her joy, kill her hope and destroy her confidence in God. Jenny made a cold-blooded decision to press in with Jesus, to feast with him. She knew that he'd said he'd come in and feast with her (Rev 3:20) and she'd have his voice in her life no matter what was on the menu.

Years later she knows this time as God's grace-filled training school, shaping and preparing her to help others walk with Jesus in their darkest times (see her book Spiritual Feasting *– Jenny Sanders).*

We know his voice so well that when he calls our name, we immediately know it's him.

John Chapter 20
I know that voice

When I'm out with my wife and we lose each other, to find her I've learnt the trick of standing still and listening. I don't need my phone to locate her, I'll just listen. She's a friendly, chatty person who inevitably ends up talking to someone and she has a tone of voice that carries over and above other noises. An operatic company had shown interest in her at one stage because of her pitch, however she felt her lack of ability to keep a tune might annoy them. Painting became her thing. Anyway, guided by her voice I'll find her quite quickly, usually engrossed in making a new friend.

I know her voice.

The Resurrection .

The events described in this chapter are so glorious you can hardly take them in. The desperate despair of the followers of Jesus turning to an unimaginable, incredulous joy is just amazing. History had changed and we still say around the world each Easter day, 'He is risen!'.

This is as central to our faith as the crucifixion, like hearing a jury pass the sentence of 'not guilty' the accused does not really enjoy the truth until he walks out of the courtroom a free man. Moreover, he walks out to find that the man who took the blame for his crimes has also given him a large bank account, a home, a family and eternal life to boot. Even more, he's standing out, alongside you, also free. We do not enjoy the fruits of Jesus' death until we walk out into the new life his resurrection brings.

The resurrection is the justification of all he said and promised. That death could not hold onto the perfect lamb of God means it's all true. Many evangelists have staked their whole message on the fact that if you can disprove the resurrection our faith falls apart.

Our life is now bound up in him, and so by him we are justified, just like we'd never been guilty. We enjoy all that he promised and spoke about in the previous chapters. He was proved right. Death is defeated, he is alive forever, and us with him (you can pause for a laugh-filled dance around the room if you like).

I want to look at two reactions to the news of the resurrection and the importance it places on *believing* in him leading to *knowing* his voice. Mary Magdalene and Thomas. Neither knew that Jesus had risen, and why would they? These things just don't happen, do they?

For one, as with my wife, the voice was enough. For the other more proof was required.

Mary Magdalene: 'I know that voice'

She was the follower of Jesus who'd been set free from a horrible demonic-infested life of sin. She owed Jesus everything and she loved him with all her heart. Whether she was the 'sinful woman' mentioned in Luke 7:36-50 or in John chapter 12, we don't really know. What we do know is that she was first at the tomb on the Sunday morning, she came ready to add more spices to the body of Jesus rather than wallow in her own sorrow (v1), and she was first to bring the news to other disciples (v2; 18).

Why was she the one in place to be the first to see him?

She had been forgiven a great deal. For her, Jesus was not just a nice thought, a positive way to look at life but a profound personal experience of forgiveness and deliverance. For her it was as real as it could get. When you're forgiven much, you love much (Lk 7:47).

When the other disciples leave after seeing the empty tomb she stayed, crying, (v10,11). This really hurt. Not only was Jesus dead but they'd taken his body as well. It deeply hurt. It mattered to her more than anything, her whole world was broken.

In her distress, she does not seem to have been overly awed by the angels but when she turns to whom she supposes is the gardener (v15) he only has to say her name for her to immediately know it was Jesus (v16). Only *he* spoke her name like that. Only *he* had used it over the years in a way that had made her heart leap and melt all at the same time. She believed in **him** with all her heart, her soul, her mind and her strength, and her name was all it took. She *knew* that voice.

That voice was forgiveness, cleansing, hope and, oh such love.

Belief in *her* Jesus had created the bed of love that was ready to hear the voice.

Thomas, really?

Poor guy. What was he doing when the disciples were altogether at Jesus' first appearing? What distracted him? Was it worth it? How many of us have missed out on Jesus because of distraction! Whatever the reason, it gave him the dubious tag 'Doubting Thomas' which is still used for incredulous people. Would he have liked that? I suspect not.

Was Thomas still contaminated with the *'let's be reasonable'* world view? Even though he's been part of the group that had witnessed extraordinary teaching, miracles, healings and demon bashing, (of which he himself took part, Lk 10) he just could not believe that what everyone else said was true.

His statement of *'unless I...I will not believe,'* is quite chilling. He needed proof (v25). Don't get me wrong Jesus had declared himself to the bedraggled group by showing them his hands and his side already (v20). They saw and believed, but Thomas wanted to touch for proof. The reason he gets a reprimand is because his belief would only rest on proof, not on the say so of others or even Jesus.

We've all been there, haven't we? We've all heard incredible stories only to find out that they're only half true. We need more convincing than listening to a group of excited people jabbering on about a miraculous moment. Do we, like Thomas, creep off back to our little world of unbelief. If you do, then Jesus speaking your name will not be enough.

He does not say believe all you hear, but he does say 'believe in me,' (3:16).

In the kindness of Jesus, he breaks Thomas open with a sentence, 'I know what you said and here, have a go'. That WAS enough for poor Thomas who falls to his knees declaring Jesus as his Lord and his God, (v28).

Where are you?

The purpose of this chapter and this book is to get you firmly in the Mary Magdalene camp. To know his voice so well that when he calls our name, we immediately know it's him. We do not require proof, we just know.

How do we get there?

Believe.

Believe *he* is fully in charge, that there really is nothing too hard for him. We know that *he* alone determines the future for us, our group, our town, our country and our world. It is not down to any government, army, person or devil. *He* alone is Lord. We *know* it.

We know that the only reason we can stand before God is *his* amazing forgiveness and love that *he's* freely poured out on us. We know that *his* plans are to spread this out across your world. We know that no difficulty, hardness of heart, opposition can or will ever stop him fulfilling *his* purposes.

We know it because it is all true, and importantly, it's true in our life.

Now we're ready to hear our name when he speaks. And you're ready to do just what he says.

'God says that what you build here will not look like anything else you've ever thought of.' It was confusing for Bernhard to hear the voice of God. He trusted the person who'd said it, but did that mean every time he thought of how to help set up a local community of believers it would be wrong?

Over time a group grew in Bernhard's hometown. The most bizarre expression of God's family you'd ever see. Twenty people from five nations and, because of its location in a tourist area, were rarely able to meet at the same time each week. It was a multinational, multi-generational hotch-potch, constantly moving group he called home. It had become family. God's family.

It's becoming a beacon for many other groups in similar circumstances. He listened, he trusted, he obeyed.

He (Peter) listened and responded, and as history shows, obeyed. It was as simple as that.

John Chapter 21
The BBQ chat

I was a nine-year-old, I remember being on one of our favourite family holiday treats. We'd hire a small motorboat on a local river. It was a tidal river, so you had to head upstream when the tide was up, and back downstream when the tide was going out. Timing was the key. You'd fill your time well and at a good pace if you got the tides right.

There were seven of us crowded into the small boat, my mum and my five brothers and sisters. I was number four in the pack, so not top or bottom. On the return journey I was allowed a go at the tiller. We'd been slightly late leaving but we just had time to be back before the tide came in. My mother had treated us to a bag of popcorn. I felt like a king, in charge of the boat, popcorn on my lap, sun shining.

Disaster! The popcorn fell through my legs. My eyes dropped and whilst trying to scramble after the golden treasure that was disappearing through the slats at the bottom, I rammed us into a soft, muddy bank. We finally got free after a long struggle, and my older brother (fourteen years old), who'd been standing in the mud, finally pushing us off. As he leapt back into the boat, he planted the oar he was using to get us free straight into my mother's eye. A huge swelling that turned black quickly appeared. My youngest brother (four years old) broke down and had to be carried home along the riverbank walk path. He wanted nothing more to do with the boat. The tide turned the wrong way, and the bright sunny day gave way to the mother of all thunderstorms.

We eventually bundled into my mum's tiny Mini Clubman in the car park, wet, late and exhausted.

I was in disgrace. I was no longer the king. I stayed well-hidden for some time.

Peter wanted to hide too

Oh, how Peter must have felt. A broken man, desperate to do something rather than just wait around. Being an older brother (because that's what they do) he probably felt responsible for the other disciples. Maybe he still thought that it was all his fault. If only he'd been loyal, if only he'd broken Jesus out. But then Jesus had risen. What did that mean? He hadn't had any conversation with Jesus since he'd sworn and cursed that he never knew him. The great protector of Jesus turned coward.

He had to do *something*.

He had to make sure his friends had some income, something to eat (v2-3), and he knew how.

His reputation of leadership amongst the disciples in tatters, he turns to his other area of expertise, fishing. This, at least, he could do.

I'm sure that the gnawing fear and guilt of the pre-cross events must be eating away at him. The excitement of the resurrection wasn't as strong for him as it was the others. The oaths and curses rolling around his mind must have been torture.

I know that feeling, and it isn't just my boat episode. I think if we're honest, we all do when we face up to our lives next to Jesus.

The night was long and empty on the lake (v3). Nothing was caught.

Not a sardine.

Zilch.

BBQ on the beach

Insult to injury, someone's calling out to them to find out about the catch. This would be normal for the local traders to see what fish were for sale, but what an embarrassment to say 'nothing' (v5). What was not normal was someone giving advice to them on how to give it 'another try'.

When the nets begin to fill with fish the other disciple (the author of this gospel) tells Peter *'it is the Lord'* (v7). Memories of his first calling by Jesus must have flooded back (Lk5:4-11) and Peter wastes no time in jumping in and swimming to land (v8). He wasn't going to wait for the boats to row and struggle in. He was desperate to see the one whom he'd so badly let down. What was said when he arrived ahead of the others, we're not told. Maybe nothing but a BBQ is on with fish already cooking (v10-13).

They'd worked all night and must have been famished. Perhaps too, a little reminder to them, 'I'm still the one providing for your needs, you really don't need to worry'.

Jesus knows our hearts. He knows when we're distraught by life. He's not in a rush and is happy to make sure we've eaten well before he addresses the elephants in our room. We know what it is, maybe others do, but so, more importantly, does he.

The Walk

We know it was a walk because v20 says that the author was '*following*' them and quite possibly overheard the conversation. He had to record it somehow. The following is just remarkable. How Jesus restores is just so different from the world we live in.

Peter's restoration takes place in the context of Jesus asking him a strange question. '*Do you love me*?' (v15-17). It comes three times. The first is in the context of Peter's own trade, fishing. 'Peter, do you love me more than these?' (v15). Do you love me more than the miracles I do in your world? The other two occasions drive the point home to Peter. It was not about 'doing the right thing' it was about love. Love *makes* you do the right thing. Love means you do *his* will.

Jesus told Peter to take care of his lambs (new believers) and his sheep (mature believers), all those who followed him. He also indicated what kind of death Peter would die '*in order to glorify God'* (remembering that our suffering glorifies God as much as our successes). He points him forward, not back. There is no mention of the denials, the bad language, the terrible use of curses etc. It's only about love.

The boat (no, not that one)

If I'd kept to the job in hand rather than bemoaning what had fallen (my precious popcorn), my family would have arrived home on time, warm, dry and happy. Taking my eyes off the task meant we were late, bruised, soaked and very miserable. The real mess up was not dropping the popcorn, which is where most of us tend to stay in life, but letting go of the tiller, losing direction.

When you get it wrong, beware of the path that simply tries to put it right. Usually something more is going on. Jesus asks, 'do you love me?' That question goes through to a deeper level than just saying sorry. Do you love me more than work, than your family, than your reputation? and so on. It finishes with '*follow me*' (v19). The restoration is not us having said *sorry*, but us 'following Jesus'.

Don't suppose we know how God is going to 'sort out' our deficiencies in life. Let him take the lead.

Listen to him.

What about you?

Have you messed up? Are you wallowing in your own wretchedness?

Well, of course, it's true, we're all wretched people, but keep your eye on Jesus and NOT on your failure. Let him restore you. Guilt never will. Repentance is doing it differently, not feeling sorry.

The question in our life, and those around us, is not how on earth we could have messed up but are we following him *now*.

We all have the same question. Jesus wouldn't give Peter the satisfaction of knowing about another person (v22). This was Peter's time, and his alone.

And to finish ...

This moment came about not as a result of worshipping, fasting or praying, as good as they are, but a fruitless night of fishing. Cold and miserable and with empty nets. As we've seen, our worst moments are his opportunities. When we've tried our hardest and got nowhere, he comes and shows us what *he* wants. He speaks, we listen.

Peter was desperate to see Jesus. He listened and responded, and as history shows, obeyed. It was as simple as that.

Peter became such a bedrock for the early church. It was not his understanding of who the messiah was that did it, but his simple following of what Jesus told him to do.

Follow me. The whole episode (see chapter 18) had been necessary to get Peter ready to really hear.

Rose sat on the bus on her way to the holiday her church had organised. She was shy and found it hard to contribute in her group. Everyone else seemed so much better at talking than her. They seemed to hear God better than she ever did.

On the journey, the Holy Spirit put a song in her head. It was a simple song that went round and round and tied in with her African roots.

At a meeting on the first morning, she shared it hesitantly. The group loved it and it became their anthem for the holiday, and helped reinforce the family they were becoming.

Hold somebody, tell them Jesus loves them.

Put your hands together and praise the Lord. (x2)

Do you know Jesus loves you? Do you know Jesus cares?

Do you know Jesus loves you? He loves everyone. (x2)

Conclusion

If this book has helped you understand the importance of listening, it's fulfilled a part of its aim. If it has helped you to know how to listen, it'll have done more. If it's made you actually *listen* to Jesus in your life and in that of your group, it has done its full job.

I hope through the book and the stories following each chapter you'll see the many ways in which God speaks; directly, through the Bible, nature, events, others (Christian or not), sermons, films and, yes, books. The list could go on. God is not short of ways to communicate, ears, however, are another story. '*Whoever has ears, let them hear,*' (Mt 11:15) is said to us all.

We were created by the father, to walk by the Spirit and, together with Jesus, be part of the community that would defeat the very gates of hell.

This involves each of us listening. Be like my little grandson with his plastic mower watching me carefully and 'doing the job together'.

It is true that we '*walk by faith and not by sight,*' (2 Co 5:7 ESV) but '*faith comes from hearing and hearing through the word of Christ'* (Rom 10:17 ESV). If we don't listen, faith and the resulting belief and obedience won't come. The intimacy with God we were created for won't be there. We will head our boat into that soft, muddy bank.

He wants to have us by his side as we cut the lawn with him with our plastic mowers. This is what it's all been about all along. Us and him, together.

About the Author

James Hodson lives in the French Alps. Together with his wife, Julie, they've run businesses, community projects, and have been involved in training and mentoring young disciples of Jesus for many years. Their passion for simplicity yet depth in our faith is a hallmark of their ministry.

About PublishU

PublishU is transforming the world of publishing.

PublishU has developed a new and unique approach to publishing books, offering a three-step guided journey to becoming a globally published author!

We enable hundreds of people a year to write their book within 100-days, publish their book in 100-days and launch their book over 100-days to impact tens of thousands of people worldwide.

The journey is transformative, one author said,

"I never thought I would be able to write a book, let alone in 100 days... now I'm asking myself what else have I told myself that can't be done that actually can?'"

To find out more visit
www.PublishU.com

Made in United States
North Haven, CT
10 August 2023

40172611R00115